# PHONETICS

By
## BERTIL MALMBERG

*Professor of Phonetics*
*at the University of Lund, Sweden*

DOVER PUBLICATIONS, INC.

NEW YORK

Published in Canada by General Publishing Company, Ltd., 30 Lesmill Road, Don Mills, Toronto, Ontario.

Published in the United Kingdom by Constable and Company, Ltd., 10 Orange Street, London WC 2.

*Phonetics* is a new work, first published by Dover Publications, Inc., in 1963. This work is based upon the third edition of *La Phonétique* by Bertil Malmberg, published in the " Que sais-je?" Series by the Presses Universitaires de France and copyright © 1954 by the Presses Universitaires de France. Working from a preliminary translation prepared by Lily M. Parker, the author has completely revised and adapted the text for the English-speaking audience.

This work is published by special arrangement with the Presses Universitaires de France.

*Standard Book Number: 486-21024-3*
*Library of Congress Catalog Card Number: 63-3495*

Manufactured in the United States of America
Dover Publications, Inc.
180 Varick Street
New York, N.Y. 10014

# Contents

# CONTENTS

# Introduction

Phonetics is *the study of the sounds of language.* It is thus a branch of linguistics, but a branch which, unlike the others, concerns itself only with spoken language and not with other forms of organized communication (written language, deaf-mute signs, marine signals, etc.). Consequently, phonetics is concerned only with linguistic *expression* and not with *content*, the analysis of which depends on grammar and vocabulary (the so-called grammatical and semantic aspects of language).

All linguistic contact between human beings presupposes the existence of a *system* composed of a limited number of elements distinguished one from the other by fixed characteristics. Constant differences between units are a necessary condition for such a system to be able to function as a means of communication. The units used in spoken language are *sounds* and *sound groups*, which must therefore be distinguished in such a way that the human ear can, without hesitation, identify and interpret the differences, and that our speech apparatus can reproduce them in a recognizable fashion. In order to be able to speak, man must learn to *contrast*, or *oppose* certain sounds to certain others.

Every act of speech supposes the presence of at least two persons: one who speaks and one who listens. The one produces sounds, the other hears and interprets them. Phonetics has thus two main aspects: (1) an *acoustic aspect* which studies the physical structure of the sounds used and the way in which the ear reacts to these sounds; (2) an *articulatory* or *physiological aspect* which deals with our voice-producing mechanism and the way in which we produce the sounds of language. The production of sounds as well as their interpretation presupposes mental activity. Without intelligence no language worthy of the name is produced. Consequently, phonetics has also to deal with the mental processes necessary for the mastery of a phonetic system and of an organized language. What makes phonetics an autonomous science in spite of the diversity of points of view from which it can be

1

approached is its wholly linguistic character.　Other acoustic phenomena—musical sounds, noises in nature, etc.—or physiological activities devoid of linguistic function (yawning, snoring, mastication, ordinary respiration) do not form part of its domain.

Phonetics comprises four branches: (1) *General phonetics* = the study of man's sound-producing possibilities and the functioning of his speech mechanism; (2) *Descriptive phonetics* = the study of the phonetic peculiarities of a particular language (or dialect); (3) *Evolutionary* (or *historical*) *phonetics* = the study of the phonetic changes undergone by a language in the course of its history (evolutionary phonetics may also have a general aspect in the sense that we can study the general factors determining phonetic evolution); (4) *Normative phonetics* = the whole set of rules which determine "good" pronunciation of a language.　(Normative phonetics presupposes the existence of a norm or standard of pronunciation, valid within a linguistic grouping, country, province, cultural unit, or social group.)

# Phonetic Value of Symbols Used

The wide discrepancy between written and spoken English makes the use of special phonetic symbols necessary even in a book intended for non-specialists. We have chosen here, among the numerous transcription systems in use within the English-speaking world, that of the International Phonetic Alphabet, the most widespread internationally. However, in order not to give to this elementary introduction too technical an aspect, the phonetic symbols will be used only when this is strictly necessary to avoid misunderstanding, and examples will be given in ordinary (English or other) orthography in all the cases where it seems clear which sound is under discussion.

The following symbols are used in the (broad) phonetic transcriptions:

[i] = the French vowel in *lit*, or with a slightly more open quality in English *bit*, German *bitte*;

[y] = the Fr. vowel in *lu*, Germ. *Hütte*;

[e] =      „      „      „   *dé*;

[ø] =      „      „      „   *feu*;

[ɛ] =      „      „      „   *fait*, Germ. *hätte*;

[œ] =      „      „      „   *seul*, „ *Hölle*;

[u] =      „      „      „   *fou*, or with a slightly more open quality in Engl. *book*, Germ. *Mutter*;

[o] = the Fr. vowel in *beau*;

[ɔ] = the vowel in (Brit.) Engl. *hot*, Fr. *sotte*;

[ʌ] = the vowel in (Brit.) Engl. *cup*;

[ɒ] = the vowel in Amer. Engl. *log*;

[a] = the Fr. vowel in *salle*;

[ɑ] = the Fr. vowel in *pâte*, or (Brit.) Engl. *father*;[1]

[ə] = covers various imprecise vowel qualities, mostly unstressed (e.g., the Engl. unstressed vowel in *about*, the first *e* in Fr. *mener*, the *e* in Germ. *Bube*, etc.);

[~] = over a symbol indicates nasality (e.g., Fr. [ã] in *blanc*);

---

[1] American English has in this and similar words an intermediate quality between [a] and [ɑ].

[ː] = after a symbol indicates length (e.g., Engl. [iː] in *sea*, Germ. [oː] in *Sohn*);

[s] = the voiceless *s*-sound in Engl. *say, nice*, Fr. *glace*, Germ. *weiss*;

[z] = the voiced *s*-sound in Engl. *easy*, Fr. *chose*, Germ. *Esel*;

[ʃ] = the *sh*-sound in Engl. *ship*, Fr. *cher*, Germ. *schön*;

[ʒ] = the corresponding voiced sound in Engl. *pleasure*, Fr. *plage*;

[θ] = the voiceless *th*-sound in Engl. *think*, or in (European) Spanish *cinco*;

[ð] = the corresponding voiced sound in Engl. *this, weather*, Sp. *nada*;

[ç] = the palatal voiceless fricative in Germ. *ich, riechen*, often heard initially in (Brit.) Engl. *human, huge*;

[j] = the corresponding voiced sound in Engl. *yes*, Germ. *ja*;

[x] = the velar voiceless fricative in Germ. *doch, lachen*, Sp. *ajo, viaje*;

[ɣ] = the corresponding voiced sound in Sp. *hago, digo*, regional Germ. *Wagen*;

[ʔ] = the glottal stop, the sound that replaces the *tt* in New York or cockney *bottle*.

Two consonant symbols written in combination: [t͡ʃ], [d͡ʒ] indicate affricates, as in Engl. *church, Jane* respectively.

Other consonantal symbols have their Engl. values unless otherwise stated. Notice that the symbol [r] is often used in broad transcription for different types (apical and uvular, rolled and fricative).

ˈ before a syllable indicates stress, e.g., Engl. [ˈbetə], Germ. [ˈhaːbən].

The values of some other symbols will be explained in their context. The phonetic transcription used is mostly of the broad type, which means that only important sound differences, or phenomena under discussion in the paragraph in question, are noted.

# CHAPTER I

# Acoustic Phonetics

**Sound.** Sound consists of *waves* which travel through the air at a speed of about 1,100 feet per second (through other matter—liquids, gases, or solid bodies—at a speed and with a facility depending on their elasticity). A wave is created in its turn by a *vibration* (repeated movement) which may be (1) *periodic* or *nonperiodic*; (2) *simple* or *complex*.

An example of a simple periodic vibration is the movement of a pendulum (Fig. 1).

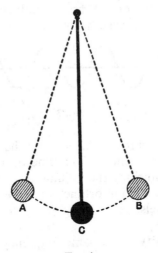

Fig. 1

This movement can in turn be symbolized by the schematic drawing in Figure 2.

The movement of the vibrating body from *a* to *c* is one *period* or *double vibration* (also called a *cycle*). The distance *de* (the distance between the point of rest and the farthest point reached by the vibrating body) is called the *amplitude* of the vibration. The line *t* is the axis of time. A periodic simple

5

vibration may therefore be symbolized by the sinusoidal curve in Figure 3.

Each vibrating body has its own *frequency* of vibration, which is determined by the specific qualities of the body in

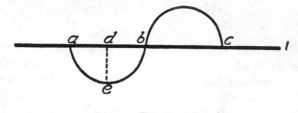

Fig. 2

question (its weight, or, in the case of cords, their tension; in the case of cavities, volume, shape, and size of the opening relative to the volume). A heavy body vibrates more slowly than a light body; a large, round volume more slowly than a

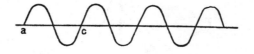

Fig. 3

small or narrow volume. The smaller the opening of a cavity, the lower is the frequency. The tone of a cavity may thus be increased by diminishing the volume or enlarging the opening. We shall soon see the importance of these physical laws in the formation of vowels.

**Pitch and intensity.** The same frequency of vibration always gives rise to the same tone regardless of the other qualities of the vibrating body. The greater the frequency, the higher is the tone, and conversely. The ear perceives sound vibrations according to a logarithmic scale in such a way that a doubling of the vibration rate is always perceived as the same interval: the *octave* in music. Thus, for our ear, the interval is the same between 100 and 200 c/s (cycles per second), between 200 and 400, between 1,600 and 3,200, etc. While the difference between 100 and 200 c/s is perceived by the ear as an octave (thirteen semitones), that between 1,700 and 1,800 (which comprises the same number of vibrations) is perceived only as a semitone.

While frequency alone is responsible for the pitch of the tone, it is amplitude in principle that determines intensity. The more the amplitude increases, the greater the intensity becomes. *Physical intensity* is measured as the sound energy which passes, in a unit of time, through an area of 1 sq. cm. perpendicular to the direction of movement of the vibration (measured in *watts*). The intensity of a vibration may thus be made four times

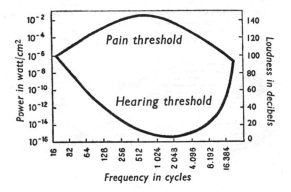

FIG. 4. Man's auditory field, showing, on the x axis, the different frequencies from the bottom limit (16 c/s) to the top limit (about 16,000 c/s); on the y axis, the intensity.

greater by doubling the amplitude or by doubling the frequency. The physical intensity is proportional to the square of both.

The sensitivity of the ear to variations of sound intensity differs greatly according to the pitch of the tone. This sensitivity reaches its optimum between about 600 and 4,200 c/s, but diminishes rather abruptly above and below these limits (see Fig. 4). A frequency of 30 c/s must have a physical intensity a thousand times greater than a vibration of 1,000 c/s to give the ear the same impression of intensity. Moreover, the perception of variations in intensity follows a law known in psychology as the *Weber-Fechner Law*. The more intense an acoustic impression is, the greater must the increase be in order for the ear to perceive the same difference. Differences in subjective acoustic intensity are calculated in *decibels*[1] (*db*). *Loudness* is the term for perceived intensity.

**Compound sounds.** Most of the sounds we perceive, however, are not simple sounds. When a body vibrates, each part vibrates simultaneously and with a speed corresponding to the relationship between the part in question and the body as a whole. Each half vibrates with a speed that is twice as great as that of the whole body. Each third vibrates three times

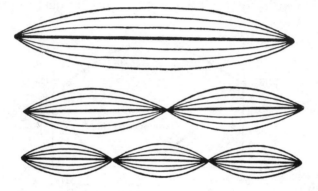

FIG. 5.   Origin of harmonics.   TOP: vibration of entire cord; BOTTOM: vibration of halves and thirds.

faster, each quarter four times faster, and so on. A cord which is vibrating thus produces not only a *fundamental*—which is the peculiar frequency of the entire cord—but also a whole series of *harmonics* whose frequencies are whole multiples of that of the entire cord.

Sounds (vibrations) may therefore vary as regards:

1. Their *frequency*, that is the number of cycles per unit of time (second). (The frequency of the fundamental determines the musical pitch of the tone.)

---

[1] The decibel is therefore a relative value, which, like the degree on the thermometric scale, must have a reference—or a zero-point—from which the ratio of intensities is to be measured. The value generally used is the so-called threshold of audibility reckoned as $10^{-16}$ watts per $cm^2$ at 1,000 c/s. A two-fold increase in intensity consequently corresponds to 3 db, a ten-fold to 10 db, etc. The whole range of audible intensities from about $10^{-16}$ watts per $cm^2$ to $10^{-3}$ watts per $cm^2$ is covered in 130 db. The maximum range of speech power is something like 60 db, ranging from $+20$ db in loud speech to $-40$ db in a faint whisper.

2. Their *amplitude*, which determines in principle the intensity of the sound (provided, however, that the frequency is constant).

3. Their *timbre*, which is due to the number and audibility of the harmonics.

If two vibrations of identical frequency are combined, the

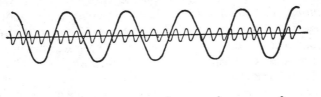

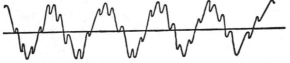

Fig. 6. Complex curve (bottom) of two sinusoidal curves (top).

result is an increase in the amplitude and therefore an intensification of the sound, provided the phase is the same.[2]

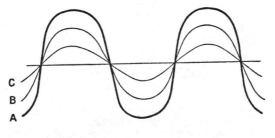

C
B
A

Fig. 7.

The amplitude of vibration A in Fig. 7 is the result of the superposition of the amplitudes of vibrations C and B.

[2] Such is the case in our example, Fig. 7, where the two vibrations begin at the same instant and have the same direction. If, on the contrary, vibration C is out of phase by half a period, the amplitude of the vibration resulting from the combination will be the difference between the two initial amplitudes (*opposition of phase*). Finally, if the relation between the two vibrations is more irregular, the amplitude will be a compromise between the two, and the result more complex (*dephasing*). For fuller details see Matras, *Le Son*, pp. 23–25.

**Resonance.**  Every vibration tends to set in motion the elastic bodies that are in the path of the sound wave.  If the peculiar frequency of the body in question is the same as that of the vibration, this body begins to vibrate also.  This is the phenomenon called *resonance*, one of the fundamental concepts of phonetics.  Any vibrating unit (tuning fork, cord, cavity, etc.) that thus intensifies an already existing sound is called a *resonator*.  The greater the difference between the frequency of a resonator and the vibration in question, the less important the resonance effect.  If the difference exceeds a certain limit reinforcement is no longer produced.

**Filters.**  It is possible, by means of resonance, to reinforce any frequency contained in a complex sound and thereby modify its timbre.  If the high harmonics are reinforced, a sound of clear timbre is obtained.  If the fundamental or the low harmonics are reinforced, the timbre is deepened.  A mechanism constructed to reinforce certain frequencies of a complex sound while weakening others is called a *filter* in acoustics.  By means of movements of the larynx, the tongue,

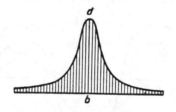

Fig. 8.  Resonance curve.  On the $x$ axis, the different frequencies reinforced with the help of a resonator; on the $y$ axis, the amplitudes.  The amplitude reaches its maximum at the middle ($b$–$d$), since this is where the peculiar frequency of the resonator lies.  The amplitude diminishes rapidly to the right and left, as the difference between the peculiar frequency of the resonator and the reinforced tone increases.

the lips and the soft palate, we are capable of modifying the shape and volume of the different cavities of our speech apparatus and thus the resonance influence which they exercise on the complex sound created in the larynx.  Our oral and nasal cavities together form an acoustic filter.  This is the principle of the mechanism of vowel production.

The acoustic analysis of a complex sound consists in determining the number, frequency, and amplitude (intensity) of the vibrations which constitute it.   Such an analysis may be made: (1) by means of a mathematical analysis of the curve (according to Fourier's theorem, which says that any complex curve can be broken down into a number of sinusoidal curves); (2) by means of an acoustic filter; or (3) by the ear (provided it is capable of

FIG. 9.   Recording (made with a cathode oscillograph) of the characteristic complex curve of the vowels [i] and [ɛ].

isolating partial tones from each other, which requires an ear that is extremely sensitive from a musical point of view).   The result of the analysis can be presented as a spectrum which can have the following appearance, with frequencies along the $x$ axis and intensity on the $y$ axis (vowels [i] and [a]) (Fig. 10).

**Formants.**   The frequencies (or groups of frequencies) which characterize the timbre of a sound and distinguish it from other sounds of different timbre (these frequencies are symbolized by the high peaks of the spectrum, Fig. 10) are called *formants*. It is now known that the vowels of human speech have at least two formants which are together responsible for the particular timbre of each vowel type (*i, e, y*, etc.).   These two formants are often attributed to two main resonance chambers of the speech apparatus: the pharynx and the mouth, though the relationship between resonators and formant structure is now known to be much more complicated.[3]   The acoustic analysis of vowels reveals the existence of other formants, some of which determine the secondary qualities of vowels (individual nuances, etc.).   Nasality is often attributed to a special formant.

[3] In fact, the formant structure is the result of the resonance effect of the whole *vocal tract* (the horn-shaped cavity from the glottis to the lips) on the spectrum of the laryngeal tone.

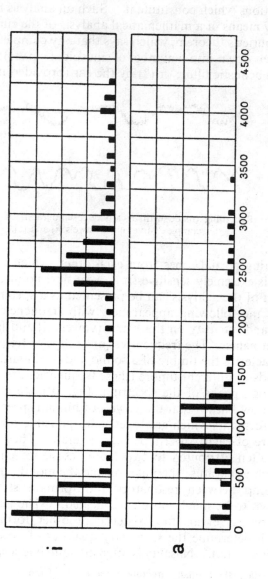

FIG. 10. (After Fletcher.)

Since the reinforced frequencies which constitute a formant—according to the definition given above of the acoustic character of pure tones—must be harmonics of the fundamental tone (whole multiples of its frequency), it follows that the formant in most cases cannot be a single tone (one determined frequency, say 300 c/s, 2,500 c/s, etc.).  The frequency of the fundamental varies in speech from one instant to the next, and often from period to period.  This is the essential difference between speech and singing.  When we sing we hold the same note for some time and then pass directly, without gliding, to another.  It follows then that a vowel formant in speech is not a single tone but a whole zone of frequencies (*formant zone*, or *range*) within which must be included at least one reinforced harmonic, if the intended timbre is to be obtained.  For example, if we pronounce an [i] at 150 c/s, the first harmonic will be 300 c/s, and this frequency will be reinforced and fill the role of low formant for this vowel.  If the vowel is pronounced at 140 c/s, the first harmonic will be 280 c/s and will function also as the low formant.  If a woman who speaks an octave higher than a man pronounces an [i] with a fundamental of 300 c/s, the fundamental itself will function as low formant.[4] It follows from this that the possibility of increasing the frequency of the fundamental is limited, if we wish to keep the characteristic timbre of the vowels.  With a fundamental of 1,000 c/s, most vowels are no longer pronounceable, because Formant 1 (the low formant) is always lower than this frequency.  Female singers who believe they are pronouncing ordinary vowels even on very high tones are in fact pronouncing acoustically quite different sounds.

**Acoustic classification of vowels.**  According to results obtained by modern electro-acoustics, it is possible to classify vowels into acoustic types.  These types are basically the same in all the languages of the world, but each language uses only a limited number of all the vowel possibilities of our speech apparatus.

Depending on whether the two main formants are in the middle of the spectrum (as for [a], Fig. 10), or at each of the

---

[4] The formants are also spoken of as *Formant 1*, *Formant 2*, *Formant 3*, etc., abbreviated as *F1*, *F2*, etc.

two extremities, clearly separated from one another (as in Fig. 9), it is possible to speak of a *compact* type and of a *diffuse* type. If the vowels [i], [e], [ɛ], [a] are pronounced one after the other, the two formants approach each other successively (the high formant descends, and the low formant rises). If, on the other hand, we pronounce the series [i], [y], [u], the low formant remains invariable, while the high formant falls respectively from 2,500 to 1,800 and to 800 (for *i*, *y*, and *u*). The vowels [i] and [y] have a clear or *acute* timbre (*i* is higher than *y*),[5] while [u] has a dark or *grave* timbre (with both formants in the low section of the register). The compact type [ɑ] occupies from this point of view an intermediate (neutral) position. All the world's vocalic systems are built on a double opposition between, on one hand, *acute* and *grave* (*i–u*) and, on the other, *diffuse* and *compact* (*i–ɑ*, *u–ɑ*), which we can symbolize by the following triangle:

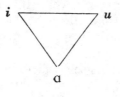

FIG. 11.

There are languages which have just these two vocalic oppositions and which therefore know only three vowels. Most languages, however, have enlarged this system by adding to it intermediate degrees or parallel series (thus, in French there are two series of acute vowels, or two degrees of acuteness: [i], [e], [ɛ], and [y], [ø], [œ]).

Depending on the position of the two formants in the musical scale, it is possible to group the vowels in a geometrical figure (triangle, square, etc., as the case may be), which, for French, has the appearance of Fig. 12.

Many languages have only a single series of acute vowels (for example Italian, Spanish, English, in which the *y–ø* type is lacking). Whereas French uses four degrees in the vertical

---

[5] Recent discoveries have revealed the importance of Formant 3 for the acute timbre of vowels like [i] and [y].

series, there are languages which have fewer or more.   Certain
languages also have series intermediate between acute and grave
("mixed" vowels, for example English and Swedish).    Finally,
some languages also have two series of grave vowels.   There
are few languages which, like French, have a separate series of
nasal vowels, characterized by a special formant and by a
certain modification of the other formants relative to the

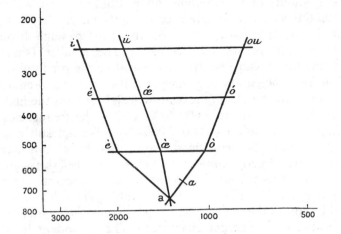

FIG. 12.   Vocalic scheme of French (oral vowels); on the *y* axis, the low formant
(F1); on the *x* axis, the high formant (F2).   (After Pierre Delattre.)

corresponding oral vowel (according to recent researches by
Pierre Delattre).

**Acoustics of consonants.**   In opposition to tones—which are
periodic vibrations—*noises* consist of nonperiodic vibrations.
Like tones (according to Fourier's theorem), noises may be
broken down into a number of sinusoidal curves.   But while,
in tones, the higher partials are by definition whole multiples of
a fundamental (the lowest frequency), there is no similar connection between the partials of noise, whence the disagreeable
impression which it makes on the human ear.   The acoustic
character of noise is determined, like that of tone, by the
number, frequency, and intensity of the partials which constitute
it.   A noise with a predominance of high frequencies has a
sharp character, while the predominance of low frequencies

gives it a grave character. The noises utilized in human language are produced by different modifications of the air stream coming from the lungs.[6] The air stream is either constricted so as to produce friction, or else stopped momentarily and then suddenly released ("explosion"). It is known that if we disturb the air contained in a cavity by means of an air current—in our case the pulmonary air current—this cavity emits a sound. This phenomenon is utilized when we pronounce the so-called fricative consonants ($s$, $f$, etc.), whose timbre is due to the shape and volume of the passage through which the air stream has to pass. The smaller (shorter, narrower) this passage is, the greater will be the predominance of high frequencies, and the sharper will be the sound emitted. The noise characteristic of the consonant [s] contains the highest frequencies of all (up to 8,000–9,000 c/s). The frequencies of [ʃ] (Engl. *sh*) are lower (6,000–7,000 c/s). We are still poorly informed about the acoustic structure of certain consonants, but what we already know permits us nevertheless to group consonants at least roughly into acoustic types comparable to those distinguished in the case of vowels. Thus, it is evident that the explosion noise peculiar to [t] is contrasted with that of [p] because of its sharper character. The consonant [t(d)] is contrasted with [p(b)] as [i] is with [u]. The consonant [k] is intermediate (neutral) in this contrast, which is acoustically a contrast between a spectrum with a predominance of high frequencies and a spectrum with a predominance of low frequencies. Similarly, [t(d)] and [p(b)] are opposed to [k(g)] as [i] and [u] are opposed to [ɑ]: the spectrum of [t(d)] and [p(b)] is diffuse, while the spectrum of [k(g)] is compact. These facts may be symbolized by the following triangle:

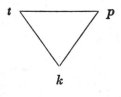

FIG. 13.

6 For other consonantal types (clicks, etc.), see Chap. III.

**Classification of sound material.** It is possible, beginning with these acoustic facts, to establish a division of the sound material of language into musical sounds (consisting of periodic vibrations) and *noises* (nonmusical sounds, nonperiodic vibrations), a division which corresponds roughly to the traditional distinction between vowels (musical sounds, also called *resonants*) and *consonants* (noises).   Consonants may be (1) pure noises (without participation of periodic vibrations), i.e., *voiceless* consonants (*p*, *t*, *f*, voiceless *s*, etc.), or (2) noises combined with a laryngeal tone and called *voiced* consonants (*b*, *v*, voiced *s*, i.e., [z], etc.).   It is to be noted, however, that vowels themselves, judging from the acoustic spectrograms, often contain noise, which is, however, devoid of linguistic importance, and that, on the other hand, certain sounds which we traditionally classify among consonants have an acoustic structure highly reminiscent of that of vowels (*m*, *n*, *l*).   There are other possibilities of grouping the sounds of language into vowels and consonants on the basis of such considerations as distribution.   We shall have to revert to these questions later.

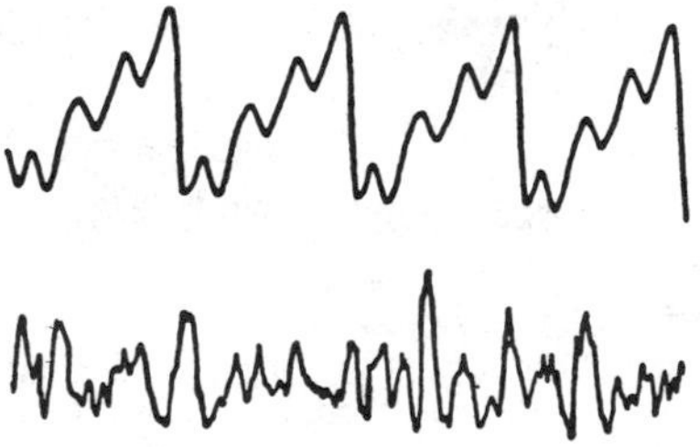

FIG. 14.   Curves of (TOP) a musical sound (periodic vibration), and (BOTTOM) a noise (non-periodic vibration; recording of street noises). (After Gribenski.)

**Visible language and synthetic sounds.** The techniques of modern electro-acoustics allow phoneticians to analyze any linguistic sound whatever and to present the results of this analysis in the form of a spectrum whose actual appearance differs according to the mode of presentation selected.   This spectrum is designed to show the acoustic structure of the sound: the partials, their frequency, and their intensity.   If we wish to show the structure of a sound at a given moment, we may

FIG. 15.  Curve of laryngeal tone (TOP) before the resonating effect of the supraglottal cavities is produced, and the same tone (BOTTOM) after certain harmonics have been reinforced by resonance.  (After Olson.)

prefer to give the spectrum the form seen in Fig. 10, with frequencies along the $x$ axis and intensities along the $y$ axis. If on the contrary we wish to compare several sounds in the same spectral graph, or if we wish to study how a sound changes along the time axis, we choose the types of presentation illustrated by Figs. 16 and 17.   If we examine a succession of speech

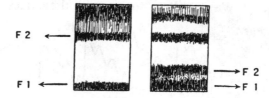

FIG. 16.  Spectrogram of the vowels [i] (LEFT) and [u] (English vowels).  It will be noted that on the spectrogram of [i] Formants 1 and 2 are very far apart, while on that of [u] the two formants are only slightly apart and in the low part of the register.  The formants situated in the upper part (Formants 3, 4, etc.) are characteristic of the individual speaker but have no linguistic value properly speaking.   (After Potter, Kopp, Green.)

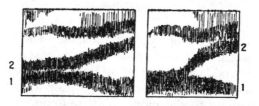

FIG. 17.  Spectrograms of two English diphthongs ([ai] LEFT, and [ɔi] RIGHT). It will be noted how the transition from the first phase to the second is made gradually.  The formants get farther and farther apart.  There is a true [i] only towards the end of the second element.

sounds in a particular utterance, we can see not only the differences which exist between the various sounds but also the changes in quality that are produced, without being perceived by the ear, during the emission of a single sound unit, as well as all the changes which sounds undergo on contact with each other. We almost always find transitional zones between the typical spectral phases. We can study, on the one hand, how consonants influence vowels, especially in the border zones, and, on the other hand, how consonants are colored by vowels. Consonants share the timbre of the vowels surrounding them. An [l] before an [i] does not show the same spectrum as an [l] before [u] or before [a]. Compare also Figs. 46 and 47. Certain findings lead us to suppose that the modifications caused by consonants in the spectra of vowels greatly facilitate identification of the consonants, and that often the transitional phases alone are sufficient to assure identification of consonants whose duration is minimal and whose audibility is small.

Since each sound has its own spectrum, it is possible, in principle, to make the phonetic differences used in speech visible by means of acoustic filters. Anyone who knows the appearance of the spectrum will be able to "read" the sound when he sees this spectrum appear on the screen of the apparatus effecting the analyses (see Fig. 58). Such machines are now being widely used for research and demonstration, especially in the United States, where the most famous type was originally created in an effort to make spoken language accessible to deaf-mutes. The invention was called "Visible Speech."[7] The machine is the *Sonagraph*. It seems dubious whether the invention in question will be able to render the practical services which the inventors expected. In any event it is undeniable that it has already caused acoustic phonetics to make immense progress.

There is nothing to prevent technicians from transforming such an acoustic spectrum, or a set of spectra, into sound again, and consequently there is nothing to prevent us from producing *synthetic speech*. Once the spectrum of a sound is known, we can design a figure identical, or similar, to the

7 Not to be confused with Bell's "Visible Speech," which was a method for representing sounds by characters symbolizing the shape of the vocal apparatus during speech.

spectrum and reproduce the sound. As a matter of fact this is what has been achieved these last few years in several institutes for phonetics and speech transmission by means of various methods, not only in the United States, where groups of technicians and phoneticians (Haskins Laboratories, MIT, University of Michigan, etc.) are engaged in producing synthetic speech, but also in Europe (London, Edinburgh, Stockholm). If the effect obtained satisfies the human ear, this is proof that the acoustic analysis has been valid. The synthetic spectra and the sound thus obtained therefore constitute a means of testing the results of the electro-acoustic analysis. It goes without saying that such results will also have great significance for a whole series of technical and practical disciplines, such as telephony and every kind of sound transmission.

# CHAPTER II
# Physiological Phonetics

Man's speech apparatus consists of three parts: (1) the *respiratory apparatus*, which furnishes the air current necessary for production of most of the sounds of language; (2) the *larynx*, which creates most of the sound energy used in speech; (3) the *supraglottal cavities*, which play the role of resonators. In them most of the noises used in speech are also produced.

**Respiration.** The act of respiration consists of two phases, *inspiration* and *expiration*. For inspiration, the pulmonary cavities expand in proportion as the thoracic cage spreads out, owing to a depression of the diaphragm and a raising of the ribs. This increase in the volume of the lungs produces a demand for outside air which then enters either by the nasal

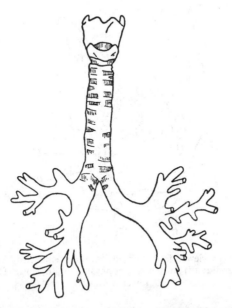

Fig. 18. The trachea and the larynx. *Below*, the bronchi. *Above*, the larynx with the cricoid beneath it, the thyroid and its upper horns above it.

chambers or through the mouth and passes through the pharynx and the trachea. Expiration calls for an elevation of the diaphragm and a lowering of the ribs, with a consequent expulsion of a great part of the air contained in the lungs. It is this air expelled by expiration that is used for speech.

In principle, it is possible to produce sounds during inspiration also, but this is a possibility that occurs only exceptionally. Such sounds are often heard among small children, and we sometimes utter them in sobbing.

**The larynx.** The larynx is a kind of cartilaginous box at the upper end of the trachea. The larynx is composed of four main cartilages: the *cricoid*, the *thyroid*, and two *arytenoids*. The cricoid cartilage forms its base, and is shaped like a ring with its setting turned backwards. The thyroid cartilage, which can be seen protruding on the throat of males, and is called the Adam's apple, is attached to the cricoid by means of the two lower horns (Fig. 19). It is open at the top and back.

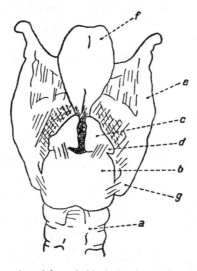

FIG. 19. The larynx viewed from behind: (a) the trachea; (b) the setting of the cricoid; (c) arytenoid; (d) muscular apophysis; (e) thyroid; (f) epiglottis; (g) lower horn.

Finally, the two arytenoids, small cartilages shaped like pyramids, are placed on the setting of the cricoid cartilage, where they are capable of movement because of a system of muscles which govern them, enabling them to glide, pivot, or seesaw. The vocal cords are attached at one end to the inner projection of the arytenoids (the *vocal apophysis*) and at the other end to the front angle of the thyroid cartilage. The back part of the arytenoids (*the muscular apophysis*) is the point of support for the muscles which move the arytenoids and control the opening and closing of the glottis.

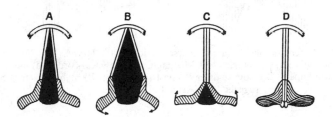

FIG. 20. Position of the glottis during: (A) normal respiration; (B) heavy breathing; (C) whispering; (D) phonation. *Above*, the thyroid; *below*, the arytenoids.

The vocal cords and the mechanism which governs them are the most important organ of our speech apparatus. The name cord is inaccurate. They are really lips, placed symmetrically left and right of the median line, consisting of a muscle (the *thyro-arytenoid*) and an elastic tissue (the *ligament*). Above the vocal cords are another pair of lips of similar shape, called the *false vocal cords* or *ventricular bands*, which have nothing to do with normal phonation. Between the two lips (lower and upper) are the *ventricles of Morgagni*, which perhaps exercise a certain resonating effect on the laryngeal tone (see Fig. 21).

**Phonation (voicing).** The name *glottis* is given to the normally triangular space enclosed by the two vocal cords (and their extension in the vocal apophyses). Because of the arytenoid cartilages and the muscles controlling them it is possible to bring the vocal cords together and thus to close the glottis. During normal respiration, the glottis is open (Fig. 20), as also during articulation of certain voiceless consonants. For phonation, the glottis must also close all along the median line.

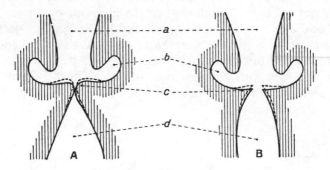

FIG. 21. Schematic plan of a transverse section of the larynx. (a) The cavity of the pharynx; (b) the ventricles of Morgagni; (c) the vocal cords; (d) the cavity of the windpipe. (A) Low register ("chest register"); (B) high register ("head register"). (After Forchhammer.)

If the part of the glottis between the arytenoids remains open, letting air pass through, we get a *whispered voice*. If the opening is complete, the glottis is ready to begin vibrating, provided the tension of the thyro-arytenoid muscle is that required by the desired register. Physiologists inform us that this tension is not produced essentially by stretching of the vocal cords, as was formerly believed, but rather by an internal contraction. For low register the vocal cord is thick; for high register it is thin and shaped more or less like a ribbon. It is likewise possible to let only a part of the vocal cord vibrate and thus shorten the length of the vibrating body, which gives a higher tone. These physiological data are in perfect accord with the physical laws governing the particular frequency of a vibrating body, about which we have spoken in the chapter on acoustics. Fig. 22 shows clearly the mechanism for opening and closing the glottis.

On top of the larynx, and attached to its cartilages by ligaments and muscles, is the *hyoid bone* which has the shape of a semicircle open toward the back. The entrance to the larynx is protected by the *epiglottis* which, during swallowing, prevents food from entering the trachea. The food canal and the respiratory canal cross each other in the pharynx. Because of the numerous muscles of the pharynx the larynx can move up and down, and backward and forward. The first of these move-

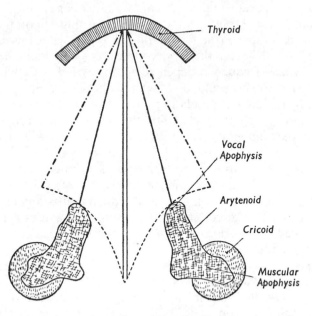

FIG. 22. The closing and opening of the glottis; *heavy dotted lines* = deep respiration; *heavy lines* = normal respiration; *light lines* = phonation; *light dotted lines, bottom* = direction of movement of the arytenoids. (After Tarneaud.)

ments is especially important for phonation, because it modifies the volume and thus the resonance effect of the pharynx.

The actual mechanism of vibration of the vocal cords is complex and poses some problems which are far from being definitely resolved. But thanks to films taken at a very high speed (up to four thousand pictures per second), it is possible to form an idea of these vibrations. The movements of the vocal cords have also been successfully photographed by using the stroboscopic effect. It has been found that the cords vibrate on a horizontal plane when we successively close and open the glottis. As the vocal cords converge to form the closure phase they meet first along the bottom edge of the "lips." The line of closure then travels up between the lips and when it reaches the top, the bottom edges are already opening again. Phase D of Fig. 20 shows the instant of complete closure. The pressure of subglottal air (due to expiration) tends to separate the vocal cords again, beginning from the bottom, until the moment when the opening is complete and the air can escape (the dotted line in Fig. 21). Consequently, the air which leaves the larynx vibrates. This is the *laryngeal tone*, whose frequency depends on the speed with which the successive closings and openings of the glottis are produced.

The possibility of regulating the rate of vibration of the vocal cords—and of thereby changing the pitch of the laryngeal tone—is in part individual (according to age, sex, individual characteristics, etc.). The longer and thicker the cords are, the slower are the vibrations. The shorter and thinner they are, the greater the frequency becomes. Consequently it is natural for a woman or a small child to speak and sing in a higher register than a man. The volume of the resonance cavities acts in the same way. The rate of vibration of the vocal cords varies between about 60 to 70 c/s for the lowest male voices and 1,200 to 1,300 c/s, the upper limit of a soprano. The average is from 100 to 150 c/s for a man, 200 to 300 for a woman.

If the speed of closing and opening the glottis determines the pitch of the sound produced, the extent of the horizontal movements of the vocal cords is responsible for the amplitude (and hence the intensity) of the sound vibrations (provided that the frequency remains the same; cf. p. 7). The variations of intensity used in speech may, however, be effected in two ways

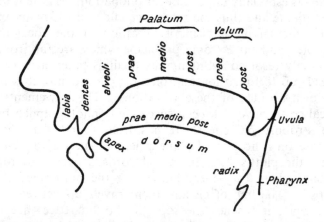

FIG. 23.   The principal parts of the supraglottal cavities with their Latin names (from which the terms used in phonetics are formed).

which are different in principle. If, by means of the respiratory muscles, we increase the force of the air current and hence the subglottal pressure, the amplitude of the vibrations increases and the sound becomes stronger. This, however, is a clumsy operation and one that is not very suitable for the realization of the subtle variations of intensity that are used in normal speech. Actually, it is also possible to diminish the intensity of the sound by only partially closing the glottis, in such a way as to let a certain amount of non-vibrating air escape. The more firmly the glottis is closed for each vibration and the longer the closed phase, the more intense the sound becomes, and conversely. This latter process requires less effort but uses much more air than the first. It is probable that in normal speech the two processes go hand in hand to produce the differences of intensity. In reality, instrumental results show a greater consumption of air for unstressed vowels (of weak sound intensity) than for stressed vowels. We have pointed out (p. 7) that an increase in frequency also reinforces intensity (which is proportional to the square of the frequency as well as to that of the amplitude).

**The supraglottal cavities.** The supraglottal cavities are the *pharynx*, the *mouth cavity*, and the *nasal chambers*, whose chief function in speech is to serve as resonators for the laryngeal tone. It is possible to add a fourth resonator formed by the projection and rounding of the *lips* (see Fig. 24). The cavity

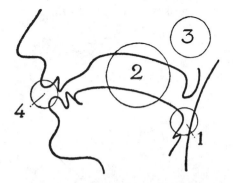

FIG. 24. The four principal resonators of the speech apparatus: (1) the pharynx; (2) the mouth; (3) the nasal cavity; (4) the labial cavity.

of the mouth can change almost endlessly in shape and volume because of the movements of the tongue, which occupies much of it and forms its floor. Its roof is constituted by the *palate*, which is divided into two parts, the *hard palate* at the front and the *soft palate* (or *velum*) at the back. The soft palate determines whether a sound will be *nasal* (air passing through the nose) or *oral* (air passing only through the mouth). The soft palate ends in the *uvula*. The shape and volume of the nasal chambers are fixed. Their effect as resonance cavities is consequently always the same. In the mouth are also the *teeth* and the *alveoli* (gum ridge, the projecting part of the palate just above and behind the teeth of the upper jaw). Behind the alveoli, finally, is the front part of the palate (*prepalatal* region).

Because of the great mobility of the lips it is possible, as was said above, to add a fourth resonance cavity and to modify the effect of the the the oral cavity (*labialization*).

The importance of the tongue—an extremely flexible organ —is so great in the production of the sounds of language that the word "tongue" is often used—in Latin, French, English, etc.—to symbolize linguistic communication in general, as a synonym of "language" (the "English tongue," etc.). Indeed the tongue is the most important of the organs of speech above the glottis. It is a complex of muscles whose base is attached to the hyoid bone and which fills almost all of the oral cavity. The various movements of the tongue make it possible to obtain all the effects of resonance we make use of in order to realize the various vocalic timbres of language and produce a whole series of different noises. A distinction is made between the *tip of the tongue* (the *apex*) and the *back of the tongue* (the *dorsum*).

# CHAPTER III

# Types of Articulation

On the basis of the division of the so-called speech apparatus established in the preceding chapter, it is possible to make a general classification of the different articulatory possibilities placed at our disposal by this apparatus.

**Respiration.** Let us begin with respiration. The sounds of language may be classified into two large groups, according to whether they are produced with the help of a current of air coming from the lungs, or without any participation of respiration. Among the latter, let us especially note the *clicks* which are rather widely distributed among many exotic languages (African languages, etc.), although non-existent in Europe and within the Indo-European, Semitic, and Finno-Ugric groups. To form a click, we close the oral passage at two points situated at the back and in front (for example with the lips and the back of the tongue). By this means we create a closed cavity, whose volume we then increase, thereby diminishing the pressure of the internal air. At the opening of the front occlusion, the external air enters abruptly. The click type may be combined with nasalization and voice, i.e., with a voiced air stream passing through the nasal cavity behind the dorso-velar closure. In *ejectives*, or *glottalized stops*, the compression of the mouth and pharynx air may be effected in such a way that the larynx, with closed glottis, is thrust upwards, whereupon the air rushes out when the mouth opens. If the larynx, instead of being thrust upwards, is lowered, rarefying the air in the mouth and pharynx cavities, and the outside air is made to enter to fill the gap, we obtain an ingressive air stream and a consonant called *implosive*, or sometimes *glottalic click*. There is nothing to prevent the formation of glottalized and implosive fricatives, i.e., by means of an incomplete front closure. Such types are, however, rare because of their reduced duration and audibility. Since all these sounds, however interesting they may be, are

29

only represented in languages unfamiliar to the general reader, we shall consider in the following description only the first group, that which supposes an air current coming from the lungs.[1]

**The larynx.** Beginning with the function of the *larynx* and the *vocal cords*, we can establish two categories of sounds, according to whether they are formed with the help of laryngeal vibrations—*voiced sounds*—or without participation by the

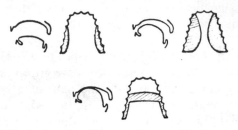

Fig. 25. Chart illustrating the difference between the free passage of the air current (TOP LEFT), constricted passage (TOP RIGHT) and complete closing (achieved here with the back of the tongue against the hard palate; BOTTOM). The figures on the left are a transverse section of the oral cavity, showing the teeth, palate, and tongue; those on the right are palatograms, made with an artificial palate, showing the part of the palate that has been touched by the tongue during articulation (*shaded area*). (After Dieth.)

vocal cords—*voiceless sounds*. All vowels and certain consonants (*l, m, n, v,* etc.) are always voiced in ordinary speech. In *whispering*, the normal voice is replaced by a friction noise in the glottis (see p. 24). Certain consonants (*p, t, f,* etc.) are always voiceless.

**The velum.** We have seen that the movements of the *velum* determine whether a sound will be pronounced with or without *nasal resonance.* If the soft palate closes the passage to the nose by pressing against the posterior wall of the pharynx, we obtain an *oral* articulation. If on the other hand the soft palate leaves this passage free, the air will escape, entirely or partially, through the nose, and we obtain a *nasal* articulation (nasal vowel if both passages are free, nasal consonant if that of the mouth is closed).

---

[1] We have already mentioned that normal speech sounds are not produced through *inspiration* (p. 22).

**The tongue.**   With regard to the tongue, a distinction is made between the *tip* (apex) and the *back* (dorsum), whence a division between *apical* articulations and *dorsal* articulations.   An articulation made with the part of the tongue just behind the tip is called *predorsal*.   It is an articulatory type which often replaces the purely apical type, usually without any perceptible acoustic difference.   According to whether an articulation is made against one or other of the different parts of the palate, it is classified as *dental* (against the teeth themselves or the region just behind the teeth), *alveolar* (against the alveoli or gum ridge), *prepalatal* (against the front part of the hard palate),

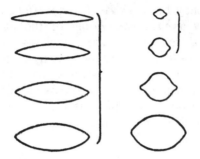

Fɪɢ. 26.   Schematic plan of the different positions of the lips: rounded vowels, ʀɪɢʜᴛ; unrounded vowels, ʟᴇꜰᴛ; closed vowels, ᴛᴏᴘ; open vowels, ʙᴏᴛᴛᴏᴍ. (After MacCarthy.)

*medio-palatal* (against the highest part of the palate), *post-palatal* (against the junction of the hard and soft palates), *velar* (against the soft palate), or *uvular* (against the uvula).   Certain languages also have *pharyngeal* articulations (executed against the back wall of the pharynx), and *laryngeal* or *glottal* ones (executed in the larynx itself), normally by means of the two vocal cords.

**The lips.**   All articulation may be accompanied by a neutral position or by a projection and rounding of the lips.   An articulation consisting of (or accompanied by) a rounding of the lips is called *labial* (*bilabial*, if both lips are used).   If the lips remain neutral (or are stretched), the sound is *unrounded*.   If the corners of the lips are drawn back, we sometimes talk about a *spread* lip position (as often for [i], [e]).   If the lips are brought together or rounded, the sound is said to be *rounded* or *labialized*. In the former case, the rounding is said to be *vertical*, in the latter *horizontal*. The latter rounding is typical of languages such as French and German, whereas English and Swedish have the former. Finally, it is possible to articulate with one of the lips (normally the lower lip) against the teeth (upper incisors). In this case the articulation is called *labio-dental*.

**Types of articulation.** By means of the following different articulations and their combinations, it is possible to modify in different ways the current of air coming from the lungs. The passage of air may be: (1) *free;* (2) *constricted;* or (3) *stopped* momentarily by a *complete closing* of the passage. Sounds produced with a free passage are called *vowels*. In this case, the supraglottal cavities merely modify, by their resonance, the timbre of the laryngeal tone. Sounds characterized by a con-stricting or a complete (momentary) closing of the air passages are called *consonants*. In this latter case, different kinds of noises, characteristic of consonants, are formed in the supraglottal cavities.

# CHAPTER IV
# Vowels

We have already seen that the timbre of vowels is due essentially to two[1] formants, of which one is low and the other high. It is supposed that these two formants correspond to the two principal resonators of the speech apparatus, the pharynx and the mouth, though this, as we have already seen, is a considerable simplification of more complicated facts. It is above all through movement of the tongue that it is possible to vary the resonance effect of these two cavities.

**Articulatory classification of vowels.** Let us take as our point of departure the position of the tongue for the vowel [a] (as in French *salle* or American English *father*). The tongue lies almost flat in the mouth, in a position very close to that of repose. It is evident from Fig. 27 that, with such a position of

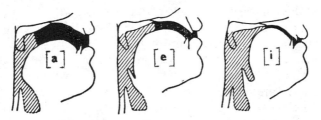

FIG. 27. Schematic plan showing relationship between different positions of the tongue (front vowels) and volume of resonance chamber. (After Hála.)

the tongue, the two resonance chambers are of an almost equal volume. The two formants of [a] are also rather close (that of the mouth about 1,300 c/s, that of the pharynx about 720 c/s). It is therefore an acoustically compact vowel (see p. 14).

If we pass from [a] to [e] and [i], the tongue, while moving forward, rises more and more toward the hard palate, with a consequent diminution in the volume of the mouth and an

[1] For certain of the vowels a third formant, as was pointed out above, seems to have considerable importance (*i*, *y*, etc.).

increase in that of the pharynx.   Consequently, the high formant rises (up to 2,400 c/s for [i]) and the low formant descends
(down to 280 c/s for [i]).   Vowels of the series [a], [ε], [e], [i]
are called *palatal vowels* or *front vowels* because, during their
production, the tongue articulates in the direction of the hard
palate.   If the position of the tongue is high (as for [i]), the
vowel is *close*; if it is low (as for [a]), the vowel is *open*.   We
say that [e] is *half-close* and [ε] *half-open*.   An open vowel is
often called *low*, a close vowel *high* (half-open = *mid-low*, half-
close = *mid-high*).   In this example we have supposed a neutral
position of the lips.   If, on the other hand, we combine the
position of the tongue for [i] with a projection and rounding of
the lips, we add a second resonance chamber and thereby
lengthen the oral cavity at the same time that we diminish its
opening.   The result of these two operations is to lower the
peculiar tone of the oral cavity, which then reinforces other,
lower, harmonics of the laryngeal tone.   The timbre becomes
somewhat more grave.   We obtain an [y] (as in French *mur*).
If we labialize the closed [e], we obtain a closed [ø] (as in
French *feu*); and if we labialize the open [ε], we obtain the
open [œ] (as in French *peur*).

If, on the contrary, the back of the tongue, while retracting,
rises toward the soft palate, the oral cavity will be much larger
and its peculiar tone correspondingly much lower.   The timbre
of vowels thus articulated becomes grave.   These are the
vowels of the *velar* (or *back*) series.   Beginning with the lowest,
these vowels are: [a] (in (Brit.) Engl. *father*),[2] open [ɔ] (in
(Brit.) Engl. *not*), closed [o] (in French *sot*),[3] and [u] (in English
*do*).   The vowel [u] is therefore the most closed and [a] the
most open vowel in the velar series.   The vowel [o] is half-
closed and [ɔ] half-open.   In French, German, and in many
other languages the velar vowels are always labialized or rounded, a fact which contributes further to emphasize their grave
acoustic character.   The high formant (that of the mouth) is
about 760 c/s and the low formant around 280 c/s for the vowel
[u] (see p. 15).   This combination of velar and labial articulation, however, is not at all necessary, and in fact there are unrounded velar vowels in many languages (for example in

---

[2] Certain varieties of (Amer.) Engl. have a similar short vowel in *not, hot*.
[3] Or in (Amer.) Engl. *go* when no diphthong is used.

Russian, Roumanian, Turkish, American Indian languages). The vowel in the (Brit.) Engl. *cut, hut* is yet another example (unrounded, half-open back vowel). The (Amer.) Engl. vowel in the same words is less open and less retracted.

In phonetics it is customary to symbolize the place of vowels in the mouth schematically by a geometrical figure which, for the most common types of vowels, will have the following shape:

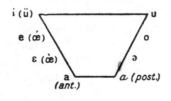

FIG. 28.

The labialized front vowels are placed within brackets. The less common unlabialized back vowels have not been taken into account.

There also exist in certain languages (English, Swedish, Norwegian, etc.), *central* (or *middle, mixed*) vowels, produced with the back of the tongue articulating toward the middle of the palatal arch (at the juncture of the hard and soft palates). Their timbre is consequently intermediate between that of the

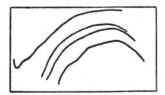

FIG. 29. Profiles of the back of the tongue during pronunciation of the French vowels [i], [e], and [ɛ] (obtained by means of the so-called *plastographic* method of E. A. Meyer). ABOVE, the hard palate with the alveoli and the teeth.

palatal vowels and that of the velar vowels. These types may also be rounded or unrounded. The (Brit.) Engl. vowel in the words *hurt, sir, girl* is central, half-open, and unrounded. The vowel in the Norwegian word *hus* (house) is central, close, and rounded; that of the Swedish *hund* (dog) is central, half-open, and rounded.

NOTE. Although most of the known vowels are articulated with the aid of the back of the tongue (dorsal types), nothing prevents us from producing vowels with the tip of the tongue or with the predorsal region (apical and predorsal types). As a matter of fact such vowels exist. The vowel phoneme [i],[4] in some Swedish and Norwegian dialects, is articulated in this way. There exists also a corresponding rounded type. The so-called retroflex vowels are characterized by a special position of the tip of the tongue which rises toward the palatal arch (cf. retroflex consonants, p. 41). The hollow shape of the tongue which results gives a specific timbre to these vowels. They are encountered in certain English areas and in American English, where they are due to an apical *r* which has often disappeared (in *girl*, *far*, *more*, etc.), so-called *r*-colored vowels.

With these articulatory data it is possible to characterize most normal vowel types by indicating their place in the mouth, the degree of closing, and the position of the lips. The vowel [i] will therefore be an unrounded, close front vowel; [e] will have the same characteristics except for the degree of closing

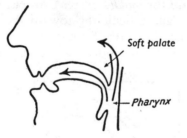

FIG. 30. Position of the soft palate during pronunciation of a nasal vowel. The oral passage is open and the air of expiration escapes through the mouth and nose.

(half-close); [y] also, with the exception of the labialization; [u] will be a rounded, close back vowel; [o] will be identical to it except for the degree of closing (half-close), etc. All of these vowels are *oral*, that is to say they are pronounced with-

---

[4] The concept of "phoneme" is treated in Chap. XI.

out nasal resonance (or, at least, without any strong nasal color).

Nasal vowels are by far less common and less numerous, at least as independent types, than oral ones. The nasal vowels in French are, for example, four in number, namely [ɛ̃], [œ̃], [ɑ̃], and [ɔ̃], i.e. the vowels most often spelt respectively *in*, *un*, *an* or *en*, and *on* (in *fin*, *brun*, *grand*, and *bon*). The nasality of

FIG. 31.  Diagram indicating the position of the tongue for a close front vowel (type [i], LEFT), and for an open back vowel (type [ɑ]). The dotted line indicates the maximum elevation for a vocalic articulation. If the tongue exceeds this limit, different kinds of noise are produced and a consonantal articulation is obtained.

these vowels is an essential characteristic which often by itself permits us to distinguish between two words. Thus the words *beau* and *bon*, *fait* and *fin* (phonetically [bo] ~ [bɔ̃], [fɛ] ~ [fɛ̃]) are distinguished one from the other only by the presence or absence of nasal resonance in the vowel. There are few languages in Europe in which nasality has such a linguistic importance. Besides French, only Portuguese and Polish possess true nasal vowels. They also occur in American languages (Guarani). In the other languages, we sometimes hear a certain nasal resonance which may be due to the proximity of a nasal consonant (*m*, *n*) or else be individual and accidental. It consequently does not play any linguistic role and is incapable of assuming a semantic difference.

There exist still other characteristics than those mentioned here which can influence the quality of vowels and thereby serve to contrast one timbre with another. A vowel may be articulated with more or less muscular tension, and in certain languages (German and English, for example) a distinction is made between *tense vowels* and *lax vowels*. Thus the long [iː] in the English *seat* is tense, while the short vowel in *sit* is lax (in narrow transcription [ɪ]). Similarly the long vowel [uː] in

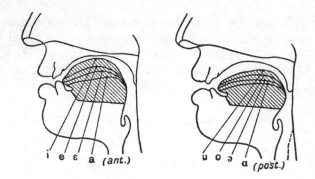

FIG. 32. Position of the tongue for the principal vowel types. LEFT, the front vowels; RIGHT, the back vowels. It is to be noted that the position of the tongue for [u] is in reality a little more forward than for the other back vowels, contrary to what might be assumed from the vocalic square in Fig. 28, which implies a considerable—very schematic—simplification of articulatory reality. (After Jones.)

the English *food* is tense in comparison to the short vowel in *foot*, which is lax (in narrow transcription [ʊ]). This is a vocalic distinction unknown, for example, in French, in which every vowel, at least in stressed syllables, is distinctly tense. Differences of this kind contribute to giving a language its phonetic peculiarity.

Finally a distinction is also made between *monophthongs* whose timbre remains acoustically the same for the ear throughout the duration of the vowel,[5] and *diphthongs* which change timbre during their emission. We therefore hear a certain vocalic quality at the beginning of a diphthong, and another at the end.

English is rich in diphthongs: [au] as in *house*, [ai] as in *fine*, [ɔi] as in *boy*, and, generally in British English, [ou] as in *go*, and [ei] as in *day*. Jones calls these diphthongs *closing* diphthongs, because their second element is a close vowel, Other diphthongs are [iə], as in *dear*, [uə] as in *poor*, and [ɛə] as in *bear*. Jones calls them *centring* diphthongs, because their second

---

[5] Acoustic spectra reveal, even in monophthongs, variations of timbre during the course of emission of vowels, but these variations are too slight to be perceived by the ear.

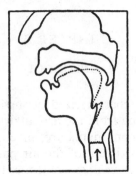

FIG. 33.  Position of the tongue for [i] and for [u] (dotted line).  (After Pike.)

element is a central vowel (the tongue movement going in the direction of the middle of the mouth cavity).

German has the three diphthongs: [au] as in *Haus*; [ai] as in *mein*; and [ɔy] as in *heute*.  Modern French has no diphthongs, but numerous spellings still bear witness of old diphthongs which have been reduced to monophthongs (e.g. *fait*, *chevaux*).

Some phoneticians (e.g. Jones) look upon the complex vowel types in words like (Brit.) Engl. *fire*, *hour*, as *triphthongs*: [aiə], [auə].  This is to a certain degree a question of definition into which we will not go any farther here.  A French spelling like *beau* (mod. Fr. [bo]) indicates an ancient pronunciation [əau], a triphthong with the stress on its middle element.

## CHAPTER V
# Consonants

While vowels are characterized acoustically by the absence of audible friction and from the articulatory point of view by a free passage of air, consonants are, or contain, noises and are pronounced with a stricture of the air passage. A distinction is made between *momentary* consonants, which suppose a complete closing followed by an abrupt opening ("explosion"), and *continuous* consonants, which are characterized by a contraction of the air passage and which can consequently be prolonged, theoretically, as long as air from the lungs permits.

**Stops.** In phonetics, momentary consonants are called *stops* (sometimes *plosives* or *explosives*) because the most important phase of their formation is the momentary closing of the air passage. With regard to English, this closing may be achieved with both lips against each other (*bilabial stop*), with the tip of the tongue against the teeth or the gums (*dental, gingival,* or *alveolar stop*), or with the back of the tongue either against the hard palate (*palatal stop*) or against the soft palate (*velar stop*). The consonants of *pike* and *bike* (*p* and *b*) are bilabial, those of *two* and *do* (*t* and *d*) are apico-alveolar, those of *cow* and *go, kiss* and *give* (*k* and *g*) are dorso-palato-velar. In most languages the phonemes[1] [k] and [g] adapt their place of articulation to the adjacent vowel. In combination with [u] or [o] the contact is velar, in contact with [i] more or less palatal, and in other cases ([a], etc.) intermediate. The degree of adaptability to surrounding vowels is greater for the [k] and [g] type than for other consonants (cf. p. 42).

We have seen that all consonantal articulation may be accompanied by laryngeal vibrations or be made without participation of the vocal cords. Stops may therefore be *voiced* or *voiceless* (or *unvoiced*). The consonants [b], [d], and [g] are voiced, while [p], [t], and [k] are voiceless.

[1] For the notion of phoneme, see Chap. XI.

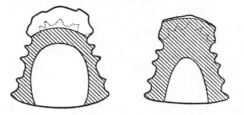

FIG. 34.  Palatograms of a French [t] (apico-dental), RIGHT, and of an English [t] (apico-alveolar), LEFT.  The striped area indicates contact of the tongue with the teeth and palate.  It will be noted that for the English [t] this area is clearly above the teeth, while for the French [t] the surface touched by the tongue extends as far as the teeth.  (After Jones.)

Every consonant may be defined according to its *mode of articulation* and its *point of articulation*.  Thus [t] is a voiceless stop as regards its mode of articulation, and an apico-alveolar consonant according to its point of articulation.

It goes without saying that the English consonants listed here do not exhaust the number of possible stops.  For example, a stop may be formed by placing the tip of the tongue against the teeth (*apico-dental stop*).  This is the case with the French *t* and *d*.  It is possible to raise the tip of the tongue still higher than in English and articulate against different parts of the hard

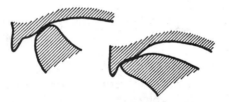

FIG. 35.  Position of the tip of the tongue for a French [t], RIGHT, and for an English [t], LEFT.  (After Dumville.)

palate (*apico-palatal stops*).  In this case, it is often the part of the tongue below the tip that touches the palate.  These types are called *retroflex consonants*.  Such consonants are to be found in Swedish where an apical *r* merges with a following *t* or *d* to form a single retroflex apico-prepalatal consonant (for instance in *kort* "short" and *bord* "table").  These retroflex types are encountered again in Sicilian dialects and in India for example (see Fig. 37).  In certain American Indian languages the retroflex *t* type, transcribed [t], is opposed, as a different phoneme, to dental [t].

There are essentially two types of voiceless stops, *aspirated* and *unaspirated*.[2] The French consonants [p], [t], [k] are un-aspirated stops. This same type is found in the other Romance languages and in most European languages with the exception of the Germanic group. From the acoustic point of view, an aspirated (English) stop is characterized by an exhalation of breath, an unvoiced noise, which is heard between the explosion and the vowel following and which is chiefly perceptible before a stressed vowel. This exhalation is not heard in French.

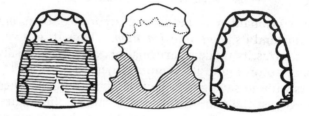

FIG. 36. Palatograms of a palatal [k] (or [g]), LEFT; of an intermediate (post-palatal) [k], CENTER; and of a purely velar [k], RIGHT. In the case of the latter the hard palate has hardly been grazed by the back of the tongue. Almost all contact is made against the soft palate.

The articulatory difference between the two types is as follows: during the closure (buccal closing) of a stop of the unaspirated type, the glottis is closed. The vocal cords can therefore begin vibrating at the moment of explosion. The vocal cords are thus already in the position required for phonation and the vowel can follow the explosion immediately. During the oc-clusion of an aspirated stop the glottis is open. There is thus a certain lapse of time before the glottis is completely closed for the following vowel. The air which escapes during this time is heard as an exhalation.

The English or German voiceless stops are not aspirated in every phonetic position. Before an unstressed vowel, aspira-tion is often weak. After an *s* of the same syllable (e.g., in English *stay*, Swedish *sten* "stone"), the consonant is of the unaspirated type.

[2] For glottalized stops, see p. 29.

NOTE. There exist also in certain languages aspirated voiced stops, for example in Sanskrit (the ancient classical language of the Hindus) and in other dialects of India. Some languages use aspirated and unaspirated stops as separate phonemes (ancient Indo-European, classical Greek).

If the aspiration is very strong, the aspirated stops tend to pass into the group of affricates or affricated stops (see page 50). This is a development that is presently taking place in Danish, in which *t* before a stressed vowel is perceived as [t͡s] by a foreign ear. By such a development the Germanic aspirated stops have been transformed into affricates or fricatives in High German (cf. English *ten*, German *zehn* [pronounced [t͡seːn]], English *eat*, German *essen*).

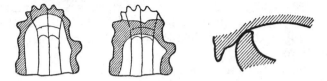

FIG. 37. Palatograms of a normal apico-dental stop (French [t] or [d]), LEFT, and of a retroflex stop, CENTER. RIGHT, shape of the tip of the tongue for articulation of a retroflex stop. (After E. A. Meyer and Dumville.)

Finally, a stop may also be realized in the pharynx (pharyngeal stop) or in the larynx itself, where it is possible to close the air passage momentarily by bringing the vocal cords close together. This is what is called the *glottal stop* and, in certain languages (German, for example), it is a normal consonant sound placed regularly before every stressed initial vowel. It replaces other stops in English in certain types of vulgar speech (London cockney *get*, *better*, or New York [ˈbɒʔɫ] for *bottle*).

**Nasals.** Since the stops by definition suppose a complete closing of the air passage, it follows that during the occlusion the soft palate closes the entrance to the nasal cavities. If, on the other hand, we combine closing of the oral cavity with a lowered position of the soft palate and a free passage of air through the nose, we obtain another kind of consonant, called *nasal consonants*. Consequently, a nasal is a stop as regards the oral articulation, but an open sound (free passage) if we consider the nasal cavity. If, in pronouncing a [b], we open

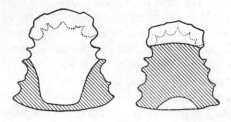

FIG. 38. Palatograms of the English (velar nasal) [ŋ], LEFT, and of the French (palatal nasal) [ɲ], RIGHT.

the entrance of the nasal cavities, we obtain a nasal bilabial consonant [m]. Similarly [n] is a nasal apico-alveolar (corresponding more or less to [d]), and [ŋ] the velar nasal (English *king*, German *jung* "young"). Other languages have a palatal nasal (phon. [ɲ]), as in French *digne*, *baigner*, articulated with the back of the tongue against the hard palate and the tip of the tongue lowered.

Since there are so many possible stops, it goes without saying that there also exist other nasal consonants. The French [n] is purely dental. Swedish and other languages have retroflex nasals, etc.

Nasal consonants are normally voiced but may lose their voicing in combination with voiceless consonants. For example in French, [m] normally becomes voiceless after voiceless [s] in words ending in -*sme* (*enthousiasme, communisme*). Voiceless nasals are not independent phonemes in European languages, but this does not prevent them from existing elsewhere.

**Laterals.** The consonants called *laterals* have this in common with stops and nasals: that the articulatory organ, the tongue, makes a firm contact with the point of articulation in question (usually the teeth or the palate). But contrary to what happens in the preceding groups, this contact takes place only at the middle of the oral cavity, while air escapes from both sides of the place of articulation. Sometimes this lateral passage of air occurs only on one side (*unilateral* consonant) without any perceptible acoustic difference resulting. The English [l] (in *light, long, call*) is a lateral type. The tip of the tongue touches the upper gums, and air escapes on both sides

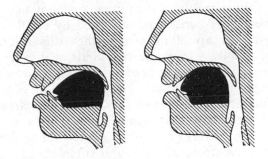

F_IG. 39. Position of the tongue for the dorso-velar nasal (English [ŋ]), L_EFT, and for the dorso-palatal nasal (French [ɲ]), R_IGHT. (After Jones.)

of the tongue. A weak noise, caused by friction of the air current against the side-edges of the tongue, is produced. In British English at the ends of syllables, in American English more generally, [l] has a dark timbre, caused by a rising of the back of the tongue toward the soft palate ([u]-position, and consequently [u] color of the consonant). Such [l] is called *velarized* (in narrow phonetic transcription written [ɫ]). Cf. also page 58.

In place of the apico-alveolar English [l], French has a dental [l] (in *lit, loup, aller*). This [l] is never velarized or dark. French, however, formerly had a velarized [l] which was later transformed into a vocalic element [u] as a result of the loss of its apical articulation. This development is responsible, for example, for French plurals of the type *cheval-chevaux*. In the old plural *chevalz*, the velarized *l* changed into [u], thus producing a diphthong which ended by being reduced to [o]. Many languages also have the palatal lateral [λ] (French *l* "mouillé"), e.g., Spanish (at least in its European form) in *calle, caballo*, in Italian *figlio, meglio*. It was formerly used in French and is still heard in certain French-speaking regions (for example in Switzerland) in such words as *fille, piller*. [λ] is a *dorso-palatal* lateral consonant, formed with the back of the tongue articulating against the hard palate. In French, [λ] has been replaced by the fricative dorso-palatal consonant called the "yod" (see Fig. 39), i.e., the English [j] in *yes*.

**Trills: *r*-sounds.** The consonants called *trills*, or *vibrants*, are articulated in such a way that the articulating organ—which in this case is either the tip of the tongue or the uvula[3]—forms a series of very brief occlusions, separated by small vocalic elements. Whether apical or uvular, the trills belong to the r-family of sounds. There are two kinds of *r* in terms of the articulatory organ: the *front* or *apical r* and the *back* or *uvular r*. The first is pronounced in such a way that the tip of the tongue, touching the alveoli, is pressed forward by the stream of air. Because of its elasticity, the tongue returns to its former position, and the same movement is repeated up to four or five times in succession for a strong *r*. This *r* is often called "rolled" *r*. In Europe and elsewhere in most languages, the trilled apical [r] is, so to speak, the primitive form of the *r*-phoneme. It must have been the [r] of Latin and Greek and probably also the primitive Indo-European [r]. This rolled [r] is preserved in many European languages, as much in the pronunciation of the

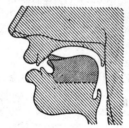
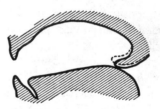

FIG. 40.   Trilled apical *r*.
(After Jones.)

FIG. 41.   Trilled uvular *r*.
(After Dumville.)

cultivated classes as in the local patois (Spanish, Italian, Slavic, etc.).   But in French, in German, and in a few other European languages (Danish, Swedish, Dutch), the apical *r* has been replaced, in modern times, or is now being replaced, by a uvular pronunciation of the phoneme.   It is no longer the tip of the tongue, but the uvula, which vibrates and forms the repeated contacts with the back part of the tongue (Fig. 41). This trilled back *r* is widely prevalent in France and Germany.

This replacement of the front *r* by a back *r* has taken place almost simultaneously, it seems, in several languages of Western Europe: in French, German, Dutch (where the phenomenon is

[3] Other vibrant sounds are either pathological phenomena or non-linguistic sounds (lip vibrations, etc.), such as the bilabial "brrr!" uttered when shivering.

less advanced than in French), Danish (where the apical *r* has disappeared except in a few dialects), Swedish (where the posterior *r* is used throughout the southern part of the country), and Norwegian (where some regions on the coast use the uvular *r*). An analogous tendency is encountered for example in the North of Italy (Turin), in Portuguese, and in some Spanish-speaking regions of America (where the double *r*, in Sp. *perro*, *carro*, is pronounced as uvular). The back *r* is also found in a region of Great Britain (Northumberland). This development—which seems to be of recent date wherever it is encountered—poses some interesting problems, which, however, it is impossible to discuss fully here. It seems in any case that this new pronunciation of the *r* is an urban phenomenon which had its origin among the upper classes of the cities and which has only slowly penetrated into the pronunciation of the peasantry. This is the case in France and Holland, for example. Phonetically this change represents a weakening of the pronunciation of the consonant—a kind of phonetic degeneration.

But this tendency toward weakening of the *r* has taken a different character in certain other languages (and dialects). It may happen that the trill as such is weakened or disappears and that the tip of the tongue, instead of producing a series of closings and openings, never completely blocks the passage of air, which continues to pass through a small opening, meanwhile producing a frictional noise. Thus it is no longer a vibrant but a *spirant*, or *fricative* consonant. This is for example the case with the normal British English *r*. The same weakening of the apical *r* is encountered in the Swedish spoken in Stockholm. An analogous change is also observed for the uvular *r*, which in fact is very often fricative. The back part of the dorsum forms a narrowing of the air passage against the soft palate or the uvula but without any trills being produced. This is often the case with the Parisian *r* (also called "dorsal" *r*). Certain open variants of the fricative *r*, without audible friction, are sometimes referred to as "frictionless continuants" (together with [j], [w], etc.). Another variety of *r* is the *flapped* type, produced with a single contact of the apex against the gum (sometimes in English between vowels: *very*, etc., and in Spanish *caro*, etc.). In American English the weakening of the apical (retroflex) *r* has often resulted in retroflex or *r*-colored vowels (cf. p. 36).

The two types of *r*—front and back—are most often two variants (regional or individual) of the same phoneme. Neither in French, nor English, nor German is it possible to change the meaning of a word by replacing an apical *r* with a uvular *r*. But there are languages in which these two articulations are two different phonemes and in which, consequently, a word may change in meaning if one is replaced by the other. This is the case for example with some Provençal and Franco-Provençal dialects.

The trills (*r*) and laterals (*l*) are often called *liquids*, a term inherited from the grammarians of antiquity. The liquids are normally voiced in French and in other European languages, but may lose their voicing on contact with voiceless consonants (as in French *peuple, pli, prêtre* with the *l*'s and *r*'s more or less voiceless). In certain languages, the voiceless liquids are independent phonemes (e.g., in Welsh).

**Fricatives.** We have already mentioned that a *fricative* (or *spirant*)[4] consonant is characterized by a narrowing of the air passage, which produces a frictional or rubbing noise as the air passes through the tiny opening formed by the articulating organ. This noise may be more or less audible according to the force of articulation and often almost disappears, especially in the voiced types ("frictionless continuants," among others certain *r*-types; cf. p. 47). This opening may be flat-shaped, as for [f] (labio-dental fricative), or it may be more or less round, as for [s], [ʃ], or for the bilabial fricative [w] (see Fig. 42). In

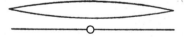

FIG. 42. Diagram illustrating difference in shape of opening between a "round" type spirant and a spirant with wide opening (on the one hand, [s], on the other, [f]). (After Jespersen.)

principle it is possible to produce fricatives at any point whatever in the mouth, from the lips to the pharynx, and also in the

---

[4] Sometimes termed "frictional continuant."

larynx itself (laryngeal fricative). English spirants are as follows: [f] and [v] (labio-dental fricatives as in *fine, vine*, voiceless and voiced, with flat-shaped constriction), [w] (bilabial and voiced, with a round opening, as in *win*),[5] [θ] (apico-dental, voiceless, with a flat-shaped constriction, as in *think, thin*), [ð] (the corresponding voiced type, as in *this, them*),[6] [s] (voiceless, in *yes*), [z] (voiced, in *easy*),[7] [ʃ] (voiceless, in *ship*), and the voiced correspondent [ʒ] in *pleasure*,[8] [j] (dorso-palatal, as in *yes*, often pronounced as frictionless). The [w]- and [j]-types are sometimes called *semivowels* (especially when they are frictionless) because they are more vocalic and in any case contain less noise than the other consonants. French [ɥ] in *lui, puis*, is a dorso-palatal labialized fricative (a rounded [j]). German [ç] in *ich, riechen*, is a voiceless dorso-palatal fricative.

As for the two spirants [s] and [ʃ] (and their voiced correspondents [z] and [ʒ]), it is customary in phonetic manuals to classify [s] as alveolar and [ʃ] as prepalatal. This difference in point of articulation is not, however, essential for the contrast

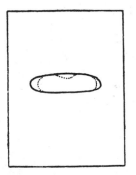

Fig. 43. Difference in shape of the tip of the tongue for an [s] (round opening) and for an English [θ] (as in *think*) with a wide opening. (After Pike.)

5 (Amer.) Engl., and sometimes also (Brit.) Engl., occasionally has the corresponding voiceless [ʍ] in *what, which, why*, etc.

6 [θ] and [ð] may be pronounced as *interdental* (i.e. with the tip of the tongue against the edge of the upper teeth), or *postdental* (i.e. with the apex against the inside of the upper teeth). They may even be *predorsal* (as Danish [ð]). These differences are hardly audible and do not play any linguistic part.

7 Both *s*'s may be apical or predorsal. French [s] is normally *predorso-alveolar*, English [s] often *apico-alveolar* (see Fig. 44); German has both indifferently.

8 Most often [ʃ] is an *apico-prepalatal* (as is [ʒ]).

between the two types. The main difference between [s] and
[ʃ] lies in the shape and size of the constriction, which is rounder
and much smaller for [s] (giving rise to a much higher frequency of vibration); in the shape of the back of the tongue
which is lowered for [s] and raised for [ʃ]; and, finally, in the
position of the lips which is neutral for [s], while [ʃ] is often a
strongly labialized consonant (particularly French and German [ʃ]). The consonants [s] and [z] are sometimes referred to
as *sibilants* and the two consonants [ʃ] and [ʒ] as *shibilants*—a
terminology based on their acoustic impression which, in turn,
is due to the difference in frequency which distinguishes
them.

English (just like German and the other Germanic languages)
also has the laryngeal spirant [h] which is heard, for example,
in English *house*, *he*, and in German *Haus*, *haben*. The friction
is produced when the air passes through the half-closed glottis.
The noise gets its color from the surrounding vowels, and this
is why the different [h]-variants have sometimes been looked
upon as voiceless vowels (linguistically an impossible interpretation). Among other consonant types we may mention the
German voiceless dorso-velar spirant [x] (the "ach-laut") in
*doch* "however," *lachen* "to laugh," articulated with the back
of the tongue against the soft palate. The same type also
exists as voiced, i.e., [ɣ]. Spanish possesses the same consonants (the voiceless form in *hijo* ['ixo] "son," the voiced form
in *hago* ['aɣo] "I do" or "I make"). [ɣ] also exists regionally
in German (*Wagen*, *sagen*). The German "ich-laut" [ç] is the
palatal counterpart of [x], in German belonging to the same
phoneme (cf. Chap. XI). Spanish possesses a bilabial spirant
which, unlike the English bilabial in *well*, *wish*, is pronounced
without rounding of the lips (in *haber*, *llave*, etc.; phonetically
[β]).

**Affricates.** Finally we have to deal with a consonantal type
which is a combination of stop and fricative. This is the
*affricate*, represented for example by the English initial consonant of *child*, and *chair*, or the Spanish intervocalic consonant
in *mucho* "much." In this case, it is a voiceless apico-alveolar
affricate [ʧ]. A similar sound is heard in the Italian *cento*
"hundred." The corresponding voiced apico-alveolar affri-

cate is the English [d͡ʒ] in *jam, John*, in the Italian *giorno* "day," etc.  Affricates also exist in German: [p͡f] in *Pfad*, [t͡s] in *zehn*, and dialectally [k͡x] in *kommen*, etc. (Southern dialects). In most Slavic languages affricates are very numerous.

**Fortes and lenes.**  The types described up to this point do not cover all the possibilities for differentiation which exist in the field of consonants.  A consonant may be articulated with more force or less force.  The current of air may be more or

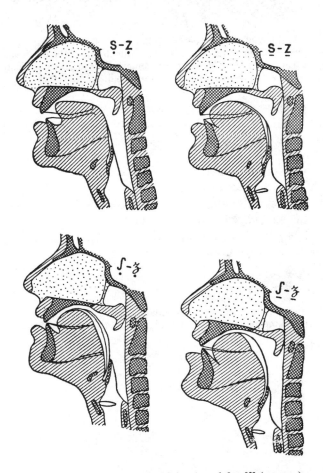

Fig. 44.    Position of the tongue for [s] (TOP) and for [ʃ] (BOTTOM).    LEFT, the apical type; RIGHT, the predorsal type.    (After Hedegüs.)

less intense.　And the resistance offered to the current of air at the point of articulation of the consonant may be more or

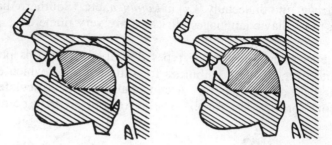

FIG. 45.　Position of the tongue for the affricates [t͡s] (LEFT) and [t͡ʃ] (RIGHT). There is complete stoppage in this figure.　It is therefore the first phase of the phoneme that is illustrated here.　The second phase is in principle identical with that which characterizes the corresponding spirant (Fig. 44).

less vigorous.　There are *strong* consonants and *soft* consonants.　In English or French, the voiceless stops [p], [t], [k], and the voiceless spirants [f], [s], and [ʃ] are *fortes*, their voiced counterparts [b], [d], [g], [v], [z], [ʒ] are *lenes*.　Among the stops and spirants, there are thus two series—a series of fortes which are opposed to a series of lenes ([p] to [b], [s] to [z], etc.).　The nasals and liquids, as also the "semi-vowels," in European languages are always lenes.[9]

[9] In English and in the other Germanic languages the strong stops are in most positions aspirated, whereas in most other languages (Romance, Slavic) they are unaspirated.　On the other hand, in the latter languages, the voiced types are always fully voiced, while in English, German, etc., they are often only half-voiced or even voiceless without becoming fortes.　So a solid distinction between the series is retained.　In French, the fortis-type may become voiced through assimilation (see Chap. VII) without passing into the group of lenes, and a lenis consonant may be assimilated to a voiceless without becoming a fortis.

## CHAPTER VI

# Classification of the Sounds of Language

**Articulatory classification.** The grouping of the sounds of language attempted in the preceding chapter has been made on the basis of articulation or physiology. We have taken the different positions of the organs of speech during the formation of vowels and consonants as our point of departure to establish vocalic and consonantal types: *front* and *back* groups, *close* and *open* groups, and *oral* and *nasal* groups in vowels, and in consonants categories such as *dorsal* and *apical, fricative* and *stop, fortis,* and *lenis,* etc. This is the traditional classification of sounds, inherited from the so-called classical phonetics of the past century (with the great names of Sievers, Sweet, Storm, and Passy), in which a nearly accurate conception of the articulations had been arrived at, but in which knowledge of the acoustic facts was still only approximate. It is this classification which has become traditional in all of our phonetics manuals and in elementary teaching. It is also from physiological facts that most of the terms now current in phonetics in all the great languages have been derived. Nor is there any doubt that physiological phonetics will render the greatest services in all pedagogical applications of phonetics (teaching of foreign languages, correction of errors in pronunciation and of dialect or vulgar pronunciation, teaching of deaf-mutes, etc.).

However, modern methods of physiological phonetics have shaken up a good part of the system established by classical phonetics. For example, it has been demonstrated with modern methods (X-rays and films) that the articulations are much less stable than was believed formerly. The old idea that a certain definite position of the organs of speech was characteristic of a sound has proved to be more or less false. The organs are in *constant movement* from one point to another in the speech apparatus (as demonstrated by Menzerath, later by Cooper and Lotz, and others). If, in the preceding chapter,

53

we have described a certain position of the organs (of the tongue, for example) as being characteristic once and for all of a given vowel, this was actually a gross simplification, made for pedagogical reasons. By processes of *compensation* it is possible to produce the same acoustic effect in several different ways. If we suppress or change a certain articulation factor, we can compensate for it by modifying the others. Moreover, there are individual and regional differences of articulation to which no acoustic differences correspond and which are consequently negligible from a linguistic point of view. One person articulates his [t] with the tip of the tongue, another with the forward part of the back of the tongue (predorsal pronunciation), without any perceptible acoustic difference resulting. An [e] can be changed into an [ø] by rounding the lips (which is the normal procedure in French), but it is possible to obtain the same effect by withdrawing the tongue a bit. The effect of both procedures is to diminish the peculiar frequency of the oral cavity. The French vowel [œ] in *peur* is a rounded half-open front vowel. The (Brit.) Engl. vowel [ə] in *girl* is an unrounded half-open middle vowel. Acoustically and auditively both vowels belong to the same type and consequently ought to be classified together.

**Acoustic classification.** The question can therefore be asked whether the moment has not come to replace the old physiological classification of the sounds of language with a classification made according to their acoustic structure (a classification whose broad lines we have sketched above, pp. 13–16). Our knowledge in matters of phonetics is now sufficiently advanced for it to be possible to make such a classification. Indeed, such an attempt has been made recently by a group of phoneticians and linguists, Jakobson, Fant, Halle, who in their work *Preliminaries to Speech Analysis* (see Bibliography) have attempted to take an inventory of the acoustic distinctions utilized in human language. Their system is perhaps not absolutely definitive, and it would probably be premature to wish to introduce it at present into manuals and elementary teaching. There may be distinctions which the authors have not taken into account. Their thesis, according to which all distinctions utilized in language are *binary oppositions* (of the type *labial:*

*nonlabial*, *nasal:oral*, etc.), has not been generally accepted, though there is no doubt that it gives an excellent tool for description. But they are the first to have attempted to use the discoveries of modern electro-acoustics to establish a new system of classifying our sound resources, and the attempt deserves credit.

We must note, however, that the traditional (physiological) classification of the sounds of language has itself not been able to ignore the acoustic point of view completely. Articulatory types have been grouped together which (although different from a strictly physiological viewpoint) have proved to be acoustically identical or auditorily related. For example, under the heading *dentals*, covering postdental or alveolar articulations, we often find apical as well as predorsal types. The velar stops and the velar nasal are classed together, although the latter, according to instrumental findings, is articulated more to the back than [k] and [g]. Normal laterals and the unilaterals are placed under the same heading. We have also allowed ourselves to be influenced, more or less unconsciously, by the linguistic function of sounds and by their differential value (cf. page 92). If all the types of *r* are grouped together, this is because, in most languages, the different *r*'s are variants of the same phoneme (cf. page 93). From the purely articulatory point of view, there is a vast difference between, say, a rolled apical *r* and a fricative uvular *r*. Thus it may be said that the traditional classing of the sounds of language is a physiological classification, modified by acoustic, auditory, or functional considerations. The principle of a classification by type of articulation has never been carried out fully—it would have led to obvious absurdities. Informed phoneticians have let themselves be guided by their ear and by their linguistic sense.

# CHAPTER VII

# Combinatory Phonetics

In the preceding description of the sounds of language, we have represented them as units, more or less independent of one another.  It would, however, be a gross error to picture vowels and consonants as fixed and unchangeable units, strung together like the beads of a rosary.  Our description of a series of isolated acoustical units was given purely for peda- gogical reasons.  In spoken language, it is rather unusual to find an isolated sound.  Language is made up of small units which group themselves to form larger and larger units.  What we hear while listening and what we produce in speaking are chains of sounds—longer or shorter—but always complex and capable of being analyzed into smaller units.  Consonants are united with vowels to form *syllables*.  Syllables form *groups*, *phrases*, *sentences*.  While grouping in this way, sounds influ- ence one another and are modified in various ways.  We have already pointed out (p. 40) that consonants are under the acoustic influence of vowels and that the vocalic spectra are modified by contact with consonants.  We are now going to make a more systematic study of some of the principal phenom- ena of *combinatory phonetics* (also called *phonetics of juncture*).

**Ease of pronunciation.**  In uttering the sounds of language, there is a tendency for speakers to try to obtain the maximum effect with the minimum effort.  This is the reason why the speaker tries, when combining sounds, to avoid articulatory movements which are not absolutely indispensable for the desired acoustic effect.  For instance if he has to pronounce two *t*'s in succession (in an example like: *at ten*), he normally does not pronounce the first [t] completely, with a closing followed by an explosion.  This would involve the superfluous effort of first opening the air passage and then closing it again for the second [t], whose place and manner of articulation are the same.  Instead the first contact is retained and there results a prolonged closure with a syllabic boundary in the middle of this occlusion (see p. 67).   In this way two articulatory movements are dispensed with: the opening of the first [t] and the closing of the second.   Here we have an example of a short cut in pronunciation, due to the contact of two identical phonemes.

If, in place of *t + t*, it is a question of pronouncing *t + d* (for instance: *at dawn*) one does the same thing, the only difference being that, in the middle of the closure, the vocal cords begin to vibrate, since the second stop is voiced.[1]   But there is only one closure.   The reverse happens in *bad taste* where it is the voiced consonant which precedes the voiceless.

In the case of a cluster composed of two nasal consonants (*in May, come now*), the passage through the nose remains open during the whole time required to pronounce the two nasal consonants.   The speaker thus dispenses with the effort of executing, twice in succession, a movement which in this case would be quite useless.

Let us take another example.   In cases like: *bad name, Bob Miller*, one has to pronounce the groups [dn] and [bm], that is to say, stops followed by nasals having more or less the same place of articulation.   The basic articulatory difference between [d] and [n] (or [b] and [m]) is the position of the soft palate.   In passing from [d] to [n] (or [b] to [m]), one simply lowers the soft palate, while the tip of the tongue remains against the teeth.   The air, which, during the complete closure, has been more and more compressed in the mouth, comes out suddenly when the nasal cavity is opened.   A *nasal explosion* occurs instead of the one which normally occurs against the gums. If, on the contrary, the nasal precedes the stop (*one day, come back*), it is sufficient to close the nasal passage to transform the nasal consonant into a stop.   The tip of the tongue (or the lips, in the case of the group [m + b]) remains in the same position.

A nasal closure occurs similarly in the case where the stop is voiceless ([t + n], [p + m], e.g., *at night, stop me*).   The only difference is that, at the moment of the explosion, the vocal cords begin to vibrate.

If the stop is followed by a lateral (groups [d + l] or [t + l]),

---

[1] At least in principle.   It may be assimilated, partly or completely (cf. p. 60 ff.).

the explosion occurs on both sides of the tongue, while the tip
of the tongue retains its contact with the gum ridge.   One hears a
lateral explosion in words like: *little*, *cattle*, and often in groups
like: *not like, bad light*.

**Secondary characteristics of consonants.**   We have spoken
above (p. 40), with regard to the phonemes [k] and [g], of a
tendency that certain consonants have to change their place of
articulation according to the vowels which accompany them.
The case of [k] and [g] is an extreme one.   But we can observe a
similar tendency in almost every consonant.   Palatograms indicate that the place of articulation of [t] or [d] is farther forward in a group such as [ti] or [di] than in [tu], [du].   Similarly
[l] is articulated farther forward in *lit* than in *look*.   In a
general way, the vowel of the syllable determines whether the
accompanying consonants will be more palatalized or velarized,
or more labialized or less so.   For the pronunciation of groups
like [tu] or [du], the tongue and the lips take from the start the
position which they must have for the vowel.   The tongue
draws back as much as the articulation of the [t] permits, and
the lips are rounded.   The result is a velarized and labialized
[t] (or [d]).   There are, in fact, as many different *t*'s or *d*'s as
there are possible combinations of these consonants with
vowels.   These different *combinatory variants* of phonemes are
unconscious and the acoustical differences which exist (and
which appear clearly on spectrograms) are not perceived by the
ear.

Each consonant has therefore, in reality, certain supplemen-
tary characteristics besides the stable qualities which differen-
tiate it from the other consonantal phonemes of a system.
These combinatory phenomena are generally grouped under
the following four headings:

1. *Palatalization:* the palatal (acute) color which consonants
assume on contact with palatal vowels (or, in certain cases,
with palatal consonants).

2. *Velarization:* the velar grave color which consonants
assume on contact with posterior vowels.

3. *Labialization:* the rounding of the lips which accompanies
consonants which are in contact with rounded vowels.

4. *Labio-velarization:* the shade at once velar and labial

which consonants assume when they are in contact with lip-rounded back vowels ([u], [o]).

French consonantism is characterized, for the most part, by a very strong tendency for the consonants to submit to the influence of the vowels which surround them. A French consonant placed before [i] is, in general, more palatalized, and is more labialized before [y], than in many other languages. The palatalizing tendency is especially strong in French. French is an extreme case among the Western languages. Palatalization of consonants is also a characteristic of Russian phonetics. English is much less extreme in this respect. German is intermediate between French and English, and so are the Scandinavian languages, and also Spanish and Italian.

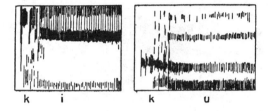

k          i               k          u

FIG. 46. Spectrograms of the groups [ki] (LEFT) and [ku] (according to Potter-Kopp-Green, *Visible Speech*). The noise spectrum (non-periodic vibration) of consonants shows up on spectrograms as irregular black lines (on the left of the figures). One can clearly see that the characteristic noise of [k] is much higher on the scale before the (high) front vowel [i] than before the back grave vowel [u]. In reality, it is a question of two rather different acoustic phenomena, although the ear identifies one with the other.

Another way to facilitate pronunciation is to suppress certain consonants in heavy clusters (English *won'(t) do*, French *que(l)que chose*). English very often reduces double consonants belonging to different words or morphemes by omitting the first (*no[t] too, u[n]known*). The omission of unstressed vowels in English is another way to facilitate pronunciation in current speech. The current English *reductions* of the type *didn't, hadn't, wasn't, I'd, I'm, I've*, etc., are due to this tendency, which has something to do with the Germanic habit of articulating the stressed syllables strongly while neglecting the unstressed ones (cf. page 82).

While passing from one sound to another, it is often necessary to execute several simultaneous articulatory movements. Sometimes the simultaneity is not perfect and *parasitic sounds* occur.   If, for instance, one has to pass from an [n] to an [r], the soft palate must be raised at the same time as the tongue starts to vibrate (or the uvula, if it is a uvular *r*).   Let us suppose that the velum starts its movement a little too soon.   One will hear a [d] between the [n] and the [r].   In this way we have to explain the presence of a [d] in a French verbal form like *viendrai*, or in the French *tendre* from the Latin *ten(e)re*. The [b] in the French *humble*, from the Latin *hum(i)le*, is due to a similar development, and similarly the Greek genitive *andrós* from *anér* "man."   These parasitic consonants have often played an important role in the phonetic history of languages.

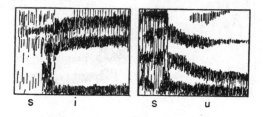

s          i          s          u

FIG. 47.   Spectrograms of the groups: [si] and [su] (RIGHT).   The formants of the vowels are clearly perceptible in the noise of the preceding consonant, which takes its color from the color of the vowel.   In reality there are two different [s], one colored by the [i], the other by the [u] (from *Visible Speech*).

**Assimilation.**   The modifications to which sounds are subjected when in contact with other sounds, and about which we have just spoken, are not of such a nature as to alter the essential qualities of these sounds.   A labialized [l] and a velarized [t] remain [l] and [t] in spite of their secondary qualities.   But it may happen that these modifications go further and change more important qualities.   When, in rapid or careless speech, the [m] in *something* is replaced by [n] before the following [θ], or the [t] in *let me* is changed into [m] [lɛmmi], and then dropped, we have to do with occasional phenomena.   The "correct" pronunciation is reintroduced as soon as the style becomes more elevated or the elocution slower.   In other cases this adaptation of a sound to its surroundings may become regular and be adopted as the norm. In English, the plural -*s* is pronounced as [s] in *cats* (after the voiceless *t*) but as [z] in *dogs* (after the voiced *g*). The ending -*ed* is pronounced [t] or [d] according to the character of the preceding sound (*liked* [laikt] but *loved* [lʌvd]). Such phenomena, whether occasional or regular, are called *assimilation*.

The assimilation can be: (1) *regressive* (or *anticipatory*), which means that a sound affects a preceding sound (the first of the above examples); (2) *progressive*, which means that the first sound affects the following sound (as in *cats*, *dogs* above); (3) *double*, when a sound approaches the two surrounding sounds (e.g., when a vowel is nasalized between two nasal consonants).

The phenomena of assimilation can also be classified in two groups according to whether the phonemes which influence each other are in contact or separated in the spoken chain. In the examples previously mentioned, we have cases of *contact assimilation* or assimilation properly speaking. When, on the contrary, certain French people pronounce *jusque* with [ʃ] for [s], it is then a question of the influence of the initial hushing consonant (shibilant) over the sibilant [s] which is transformed into a hushing consonant [ʃ]. This is a case of *distant assimilation* or *dilation*. An example of dilation is also the replacement of *cerch(i)er*, beginning with [s], with modern French *chercher* (with [ʃ]).

Distant assimilation especially affects vowels. If, in French, one often hears the unstressed palatal vowel in *vous aimez* more close than in *nous aimons* ([eme] but [ɛmɔ̃]), we must explain the close nature of the first vowel in *aimez* by regressive assimilation from the second vowel. In the same way, if the vowel *ê* is more close in *têtu* than in *tête*, one must see the effect of the regressive action of the final close [y]. This vocalic dilation is sometimes called *metaphony*. In certain cases, we also use the German term *umlaut*. If, in certain German plurals (as *Söhne* of *Sohn* "son," *Bücher* of *Buch* "book"), there is a palatal vowel, while the stem has a velar vowel, we explain this change by the fact that formerly there was an [i] (palatal element) in the ending which, through a regressive assimilation, has transformed the velar vowel into a palatal vowel. There are also traces of the old Germanic umlaut in such English plurals as, for instance, *men* from *man*, *geese* from *goose*, *feet* from *foot*.

In certain languages, this vocalic dilation plays a great role in the paradigms of substantives and of verbs. The Turkish plural is in *-lar* or in *-ler* according to whether the stem contains a velar vowel or a palatal vowel. The plural of *at* (horse) is *atlar*, that of *gül* (rose) is *güller*. The Finnish ablative is in *-lta* or *-ltä* according to whether the stem has a back or front vowel (*asemalta* "from the station," but *järveltä* "from the lake"). We call these phenomena *vowel harmony* or *vocalic harmony*. They are particularly characteristic of the Uralic and Altaic languages.

**Dissimilation and differentiation.** The assimilative tendency is, so to speak, a negative force in the life of languages. It tends to reduce the differences between phonemes as much as possible. It is evident that if this tendency could act freely, it would end by reducing to zero the distinctions between phonemes, distinctions which are indispensable for comprehension, and which presuppose phonetic differences. If the effects of assimilation threaten important distinctions, it often happens that the language reacts in such a way as to reestablish the indispensable differences or even to accentuate still more the individuality of the phonemes. In reality, the sounds that we actually pronounce are the result of a compromise between the assimilative tendency—human laziness, if you wish to call it that—and the necessity to make oneself understood.

A phonetic change which results in a sharpening of the differences between two phonemes is called *dissimilation*, if the phonemes concerned are separated by others, *differentiation*, if the two phonemes are in contact. Dissimilation sometimes serves to avoid an annoying repetition of two identical phonemes. It is in this way that one must explain the vulgar French *colidor* instead of the correct word *corridor*; or the modern French *couloir* for the older form *couroir*, the Spanish *árbol* (tree) from the Latin *arbor*, etc. English *heaven* (cf. German *Himmel*) is the result of a change of [m] to [v] because of the final nasal, while the German form represents a change of the final *-n* into *-l* for a corresponding reason. The original form for both was *himin*. English *marble* is due to a French

*marbre* whose second *r* was changed into *l*.   These are phenomena of dissimilation.   There is, on the other hand, differentiation in the treatment of the former French diphthong *ei* in *mei*
(mod. French *moi* [mwa]), *rei* (mod. French *roi* [rwa]) which
was transformed into *oi* (pronounced at first like [ɔi]).   The
two elements of the diphthong have become more and more
distant one from the other as far as timbre is concerned.   It is
through a similar development that the German *ei* (of *mein*
"my," *Bein* "leg," etc.) has come to be pronounced as [ai].
In numerous cases, the English diphthongs [ai] and [au] are
due to a similar development though the spelling obscures the
phonetic facts (*mine, fine, house, out,* etc.).

**Inversion, metathesis.**   It happens, at times, that the phonemes change places in the spoken chain.   If the phonemes
which change places are in contact, this is called *inversion*.   If
the phonemes are separated, it is called *metathesis*.   Sometimes
both phenomena are called metathesis.   There is inversion
when the Latin *formaticum* gives *fromage* in French and when
the proper name of *Roland* takes in Italian the form of *Orlando*.
There is metathesis in the vulgar Spanish form *flaire* for *fraile*
(monk), or in the vulgar, dialectal, or childish French *mazaguin*
for *magasin*.   Metathesis is frequent in the language of children.   The liquids (*r* and *l*) often change places in relation to the
vowel.   The Latin *periculum* has become *peligro* in Spanish
(metathesis of an intermediary form *periglo*); in the same way
*miraculum* has become *milagro*, etc.

**Haplology.**   If, in the spoken chain, one limits oneself to
articulating a group of phonemes once which should be articulated twice in succession, this is called *haplology* or *hapaxepy*.
In a few words, such a pronunciation has become established
and accepted as correct (Latin *stipendium* for *stipipendium*, the
linguistic term *morphonology* for *morphophonology*).   It is
through some kind of haplology that one explains the English
adverbs of the type of *probably* from *probable* (for *probable-ly*).

**Sandhi.**   When the phenomena of combinatory phonetics of
which we have just spoken are produced through the combination of words in a sentence (when, for instance, the [ð] in

*both these* becomes more or less voiceless), one speaks of *sandhi*, a term borrowed from the ancient Hindu grammarians, which signifies *junction, union*. Sandhi phenomena were particularly frequent in the ancient language of India (Sanskrit) but are also characteristic of certain modern languages (Russian, for example). A great number of examples are also found in French (particularly assimilation of voice in consonants).

**Synchronic phenomena and diachronic phenomena.** It is important, in speaking of the phenomena of combinatory phonetics, to make a distinction between the phenomena which occur within a phonetic system in consequence of the habits peculiar to the language in question, and combinatory phenomena which are developments in the evolution of language. Combinatory habits are different from one language to another. If, in French, one combines a consonant at the end of a syllable with a consonant beginning the following syllable (the group [-tl-] in *vous êtes là*), the final consonant is assimilated. In our example, the [t] becomes voiced. If one makes the same combination [-tl-] in Swedish (*ett litet barn* "a little child"), the [l] is assimilated by the [t] and becomes somewhat voiceless. In Germanic languages (English, German, Swedish, etc.), the voiceless consonant normally assimilates the voiced consonant. In French it is sometimes one, sometimes the other, according to the place occupied by the consonant in the syllable. Those are examples of *combinatory* rules. Combinatory phenomena of this kind are *synchronic phenomena*.

If, on the other hand, the Latin *formaticum* has become *fromage* in French, or if the Latin *miraculum* has given in Spanish *milagro*, we are dealing with a phonetic change which has been produced in the course of the centuries, and is called a *historic* (or *diachronic*) *phenomenon*. Such phonetic changes have often begun as combinatory phenomena—even through real errors in pronunciation (*lapsus linguae*)—which, for one reason or another, have become fixed and ended by becoming stabilized. These are problems to which we will have to return.

**The syllable.** Several times we have stressed the fact that sounds are grouped in larger units. The most important of these units is the *syllable*.   It is one of the fundamental notions of phonetics.   If phoneticians are not always in agreement about defining a syllable, it is partly because different points of view have been chosen for its definition (acoustic, articulatory, functional), partly because the apparatus which has been used up to now has not enabled phoneticians to locate the boundaries of syllables on the graphs or tracings obtained. But it would be an error to conclude that the syllable as a phonetic phenomenon does not exist and that the grouping of phonemes in syllables is a mere convention without any objective reality (a view held, for example, by Panconcelli-Calzia, von Essen).   Even a person without any linguistic training usually has a very clear idea of the number of syllables in a spoken chain.   The very fact that versification is so often based on the number of syllables (for instance in French) furnishes us with proof that the syllable is a phonetic unit of which a speaker is perfectly aware.   The question for the phonetician is to try to find the acoustic and articulatory reality which is at the base of this grouping of sounds into syllables.

A syllable which ends in a vowel is called *open*, and a syllable where the vowel is followed by one or more consonants is called *closed*.   In the word *Monday*, the first syllable (*mon-*) is closed, the second is open.

According to traditional opinion a syllable consisted of a vowel forming the *support* or *nucleus*, surrounded by consonants.   (Hence the name consonant = which *sounds with* something, which cannot sound alone.)   The vowels are also called *sonants*, because they can sound without the support of anything else.   This is a functional conception of the syllable and of the concepts of vowel and consonant.   According to this definition, the [r] of the Czech *krk* (neck) is a vowel, because it functions as syllabic nucleus.   The syllabic [l] of the English *little*, *bottle*, is also a vowel, because it constitutes a syllable by itself.   We are also forced to classify the [s] of the interjection *pst* as a vowel, because it has in this case the function of syllabic support.   With this definition of the syllable, of vowels and consonants, we are obliged to classify as a vowel any phoneme which in a given case plays the role of syllabic nucleus, and in the group of consonants any phoneme which does not have this role.   We are then obliged to define the syllable and also vowels and consonants differently according to the language under study.   This is, indeed, what should be done.   Each language has its own rules for grouping its phonemes into syllables.   The same group which in one language is pronounced in a single syllable, must necessarily be pronounced as two syllables in another.   In Swedish, loan-words in *-oir* from French (*lavoir*, *boudoir*, etc.) are pronounced with a dissyllabic group [-uaːr] (*lavoir* in Swedish has three syllables), because Swedish does not possess [u] as a consonant and Swedish consequently automatically makes two syllables of a succession [u + ɑ].   A Japanese is inclined to hear European words like *club*, *film* as three-syllabic, because his language does not combine consonants into monosyllabic clusters and admits only open syllables.

But this sort of functional (structural) definition of the syllable does not free us from the necessity of determining what characterizes this unit in sound waves and in articulation and of discovering what happens when we pass from one syllable to the next.

The Danish phonetician Otto Jespersen saw a decisive factor for the constitution of syllabic structure in the tendency of sounds to group themselves according to their sonority (or their audibility).   According to Jespersen, phonemes group around the most sonorous phoneme (often, but not always, a vowel) according to their degree of sonority.   Jespersen has classified sounds according to their degree of sonority in the following manner (beginning with the least sonorous):

1.   Voiceless consonants:
    a.   Stops (*p*, *t*, *k*);
    b.   Fricatives (*f*, *s*, etc.);
2.   Voiced stops (*b*, *d*, *g*);
3.   Voiced fricatives (*v*, *z*, etc.);
4.   Nasals and laterals (*m*, *n*, *l*, etc.);
5.   Trills and flaps (*r*);
6.   Close vowels (*i*, *y*, *u*);
7.   Semi-close (mid) vowels (*e*, *o*, ɛ, ɔ, etc.);
8.   Open vowels (*a*, etc.).

Syllables of the type of *plain*, *freight*, *like* are consequently in accordance with Jespersen's diagram.   A syllable according to this phonetician would be the *distance between two minima of sonority*. But actually there are syllables which are in contradiction to Jespersen's diagram. The Latin *stare* is proof of this, since the [s] is a little more sonorous than the [t] and the word, nevertheless, contains only two syllables. The French *strict* is another example. The Germanic and Slavic languages have numerous initials of this kind and offer even more striking examples of exceptions to Jespersen's rule. The Swedish *spotskt* ("in an arrogant manner") would consist of three syllables if analyzed in terms of the sonority of phonemes, while it actually contains only one syllable.

On the other hand, it is evident that in many languages there is a very clear tendency to bring the structure of the syllable as close as possible to the ideal described by Jespersen. The Latin *stare* has been transformed into *istare* or *estare* by the addition of an *epenthetic* vowel which renders the group *sta* dissyllabic. The Spanish *estar* goes back to this form and also the old French *ester* (whence the modern past participle *été*, after the fall of the preconsonantal *s*). This development thus has made the syllabic structure of the word conform more to the ideal. Jespersen's theory, which has been accepted by the English phonetician Daniel Jones among others, is a good description of the ideal syllable, but it does not tell us what is in all circumstances essential in a syllable. Nor does it tell us where the boundary between syllables is to be found, namely, what we call the *syllabic boundary*.

It appears clearly from the table above that the grouping of sounds according to their sonority is also, basically, a grouping according to the degree of opening. A vowel is more sonorous and also more open than a consonant, a stop is more closed (and less sonorous) than a fricative, an [a] is more open and more sonorous than an [i], etc. The Swiss linguist Ferdinand de Saussure had already formulated, independently of Jespersen, a definition of the syllable based on the degree of opening of the sounds. According to him, consonants are grouped around vowels according to their degree of opening. The syllabic boundary is at the junction of a more close sound and one more open. It is consequently possible, at least in certain cases, to determine from this definition of the syllable, the place of the syllabic boundary which, in many languages, plays an important role.

Saussure called the opening occurring at the beginning of the syllable the *explosion*, and the closing at the end, the *implosion*. This terminology is still used in many modern treatises on phonetics, where one calls *implosive* any consonant which is placed after the vocalic nucleus (the vowel) of the syllable, and *explosive* any consonant which is placed in front of the vowel. According to Saussure, a syllable may be symbolized by the sign < > (opening + closing). Wherever one finds > < (closing + opening) there is a syllabic boundary.

The French phonetician Maurice Grammont and, after him, Pierre Fouché, have defined the syllable in physiological terms. The syllable is characterized, according to these scholars, by a *growing tension* of the muscles of the voice-producing mechanism, followed by a *decreasing tension*. Articulation is thus more energetic at the beginning of the syllable and decreases gradually from the vowel on. One can, with Fouché, characterize the syllable by the following diagram:

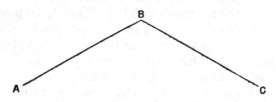

FIG. 48. The line A–B symbolizes the increasing tension of the syllable, the line B–C the decreasing tension. The point B is the culminating point of the syllable.

It is evident that the syllabic theory of Grammont and Fouché contains something essential regarding the solution of the problem of the syllable. It is confirmed by a great number of facts from historical phonetics, which go to show that implosive[2] consonants weaken or disappear more easily than the explosives,[2] whose articulation is more energetic and resists destructive forces (assimilation, opening, vocalization) much better. This theory has also been confirmed recently by results obtained in the field of acoustic phonetics.

The American phonetician Stetson, who measured the action of the respiratory muscles and believed that he had established

[2] According to the terminology quoted above.

the existence of a relationship between syllables and the inner-
vation of the respiratory muscles, also compared the curves of
these musculatory variations with the curves of sonorous intensity.   There seemed to be a perfect correspondence.   In the
course of the production of the syllable, the sonorous intensity
increased and decreased along with the variations of the
activity of the respiratory muscles.   Later scholars have, however, looked upon Stetson's results with some scepticism.   The
curves of intensity obtained by the German E. Zwirner and
later phoneticians also show a fairly good correspondence
between the maxima of intensity and the syllables.

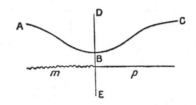

FIG. 49.  Kymographic recording of a group *um/pu* (according to Fouché).
The top line (A–B–C) shows the tension of the laryngeal muscles.   The hori-
zontal line is the nasal curve (nasal vibrations for the *m*, no vibrations for the *p*).
The vertical line D–E is the syllabic boundary.

These  acoustic  notions  are  easily  reconcilable  with  the
physiological theory of the French phoneticians.   If the tension
of the muscles of the larynx and the mouth increases, this
increase is expressed acoustically by a strengthening of the intensity of the sounds which are produced.   The sonorous
intensity increases with the tension of the muscles.   Stetson,
who has also measured the pressure of the lips and of the tongue
as well as the pressure of the air in the mouth, has found a
stronger pressure at the beginning of the syllable, and a weaker
pressure toward the end.   This is also true for subglottal
pressure (according to Strenger).   These results are perfectly
reconcilable with the idea of variations of muscular tension in
its entirety.   Later results obtained by the author of this book
seem to indicate a difference of mutual acoustic influence
between vowel and consonant as a possible cue to the syllabic
boundary perceived.

**The word, the group, the phrase.** If one asks a non-linguist which is the next higher unit into which syllables in their turn are grouped, he will probably answer that it is the *word*. But it is important to realize that the word is not a phonetic unit in the first place. While the number of syllables of a pronounced sentence can be determined solely with the help of phonetic criteria, without troubling about the meaning of the statement, it is necessary, in order to analyze the sentence into words, to

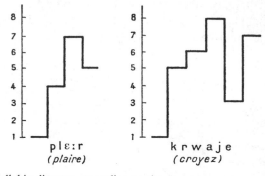

FIG. 50.   Syllabic diagram, according to the Jespersen system, of two French words: *plaire* [plɛːr] and *croyez* [krwaje].   Each summit represents a syllable, independently of its absolute level.   The words are thus respectively of one and two syllables.

know their meaning also.   The word is a unit of the linguistic *content*, not of the *expression*.   It is a *semantic* unit and not a *phonetic* unit.   A Frenchman who hears a group like *lavoir* will say immediately that this group contains two syllables, but he needs to hear it in a context to know whether it is a question of one or of two words (of *la voir* or *l'avoir* or *lavoir*).   A person who does not know French, and who hears a group like *je l'ai vu* ([ʒlevy]) pronounced, will probably hear the number of syllables within it but he will be absolutely unable to tell us the number of words, as long as he does not understand the meaning.

In reality the *phonetic group* is the higher unit that we are looking for.   In English, as well as in French, the phonetic group is determined by the presence of stress on one of the syllables, in French the last one; in English its position is free (see p. 82).   In English, as in other Germanic languages, any word of importance in the sentence—noun, verb, adjective, adverb—has a stress and is the center of a group to which often belong a number of auxiliary words (articles, pronouns, auxiliary verb forms, conjunctions, etc.). Compare the following examples with two groups (two stressed syllables): *a déad mán, the gírl is sínging*; with three: *Lóndon is an óld cíty*, etc. In French, the system is very different. If we say in French *un enfant*, there is only one tonic stress (on *-fant*). It is one single phonetic group. If we say *un enfant pauvre*, there will still be a single stress on *pauv-* but no more stress on *-fant*. It will still be a single group. This is a peculiarity of the phonetics of French as opposed to English. The word loses its own stress and is dominated by the accent of the group. In a similar case, English would use two stresses, one on the adjective and one on the substantive (*a póor chíld*). If, on the other hand, we say *l'enfant joue*, there will be two stresses and consequently two groups. There is, in French, less correspondence between the phonetic unit we call the group, and the semantic unit which is the word, than, for instance, in the Germanic languages.

The phonetic groups in turn form *phrases*, the length of which is governed by the process of breathing and the interruptions necessary for an intake of breath (*breath groups*). The length of the respiratory phrases varies a great deal according to individuals and to the nature of what is said. The teaching of diction has among its aims the development of good breathing habits. Students are taught to make the respiratory pauses coincide with the natural pauses called for by the text, that is, to make the breath groups coincide with syntactical units. The art of speaking well, to a great extent, consists of creating as perfect a correspondence as possible between the content and the expression (the meaning and the sounds).

**The articulatory basis.** The term *articulatory basis* is often applied as a convenient, but not strictly scientific label for all the articulatory habits which characterize a language. We have already given examples of the considerable differences between languages in this respect. One language has a predilection for front articulations (dentals, apicals, palatals), another for back articulations (velars, pharyngeals, laryngeals). In several languages the lips play a great part and rounding of the lips is employed to distinguish one vocalic timbre from another. In such cases labialization, when used, is very strong. In other languages, very little use is made of the lips, and when used, the labialization is very weak. There are languages where the consonants come under very strong influence from the vowels. There are others where this influence is restricted. Certain languages have an energetic articulation, while others are characterized by a relaxed articulation which often results in a tendency to diphthongize the vowels. The articulatory peculiarities referred to with the traditional term articulatory basis are essentially of this kind.

If, to give a concrete example, we compare the French articulatory basis with that of English, we can see that these two languages are, from the phonetic point of view, diametrically opposed. All French pronunciation is characterized by a tendency towards a front articulation. The *t*'s, *d*'s, *n*'s are pure dentals. The consonants easily become palatalized in a palatal setting. A few vowels, of the back series, have a tendency to advance their place of articulation in the mouth ([u] and [ɔ]). The French phonetic system is also dominated by labial articulation. The language has a complete series of rounded front vowels. And labialization, when it takes place, is very strong and takes the form of a real (horizontal) rounding of the lips, and not simply of a slight amount of projection. There are no mixed vowels. The whole articulation is tense and energetic. Vowels have a precise timbre and show no tendency towards diphthongization. The expiratory accent (see p. 80) is weak, and the unstressed syllables are almost as clearly articulated as the stressed syllables. There are no lax vowels. Nasalization of the nasal vowels is very strong and makes a sharp contrast between the nasal vowels and the oral ones. The word loses its phonetic individuality in the sentence.

English, on the contrary, is characterized by a tendency to move the articulations back in the mouth. The *t*'s, *d*'s, *n*'s are alveolar. The consonants become relatively little palatalized in a palatal setting. The velar vowels are clearly back. Labialization is very weak and entails only a certain amount of projection of the lips. There is no labial front series. There are, on the other hand, mixed vowels. The articulation is lax and diphthongs are numerous. Certain (long) monophthongs tend to become diphthongs. The expiratory accent is strong and the unstressed syllables are very weakly articulated, so that their vowel inventory tends to be reduced to a neutral vowel (*vocal murmur*). The short vowels are lax as compared with the long ones. There are no really nasal vowels, only nasalization or, particularly in certain limited regions of the United States, a tendency to nasalize the whole articulation ("nasal twang"). The English word, much more than the French, keeps its phonetic independence in the sentence, where all the full words (substantives, adjectives, adverbs, verbs) have their own accent.

It is therefore not surprising that English-speaking people often pronounce French badly just as the Frenchman pronounces English badly. Their articulatory bases are very different, sometimes directly opposed.

# CHAPTER VIII
# Quantity

The sounds of language can be distinguished from one another not only by qualitative differences but also by their *duration* (extension in time) or *length*. All sounds, with the exception of stops, may be prolonged as long as the pulmonary air allows. And the stops themselves are capable of a certain lengthening, since the closing can be prolonged within certain limits. We can also call this duration of sounds their *quantity*. There is a whole series of factors which together determine the quantity of each phoneme.

**Objective (measurable) quantity.** The duration of a concrete sound articulated at a certain moment in a given context (let us say the [t] of *alter* in a sentence pronounced in front of the mouthpiece of a recording kymograph) can be measured on a graph in hundredths of a second. We can also calculate the duration of a great number of *t*'s in the same context or in different contexts, with a single individual or with several individuals, and calculate the average. Or else we can compare the average of a great number of *t*'s with the same average for *d*'s or *k*'s, etc. We can compare the duration of [i] before [t] and that of [i] before [s], or the average duration of [i] in a given position with that of [a] in the same position, and thus arrive at average figures for each phoneme and for each position. If we establish that the [t] in our example given above has lasted four hundredths of a second, we are dealing with an *absolute* quantity. If, on the other hand, we establish that an [i], in a given position, is always shorter than an [a], or that the same vowel is longer before [s] than before [t], we are dealing with *relative* duration.

Instrumental examination of the variations of duration of speech sounds has shown interesting differences. First, it is to be noted that the quantity of each sound depends on the speed of delivery. The faster we speak, the more each sound is

shortened, and conversely.   Thus, the duration of sounds depends on the length of the group pronounced.   The longer this
is, the shorter each sound becomes.   But the durations of
speech sounds depend also on their own phonetic qualities.
Let us give a few examples of the rules which thus determine
the quantity of sounds and which seem to be nearly general in
all languages.   These rules are to a great extent due to research
done in a great number of languages by the late E. A. Meyer.

The more close (higher) a vowel is, the shorter is its duration,
all other conditions being equal.   An [i] is shorter than an [e],
and an [ɛ] shorter than an [a].   The back vowels are often
shorter than the corresponding front vowels.   The diphthongs
are longer than the monophthongs.   An English short [i]
before [t] shows a mean quantity of 13.9 c/s, [ə] a mean of
20.1, the vowel [æ] in *man* 22.4.   For a long [i] and a long [ɑ]
(before [t]) the figures are respectively 20.1 and 29.2 (all figures
refer to British English).

Furthermore, the vocalic quantity depends also on the consonant which follows.   A vowel is longer in front of a fricative
than in front of a stop, and longer in front of a voiced consonant
than in front of a voiceless one.   Nasal consonants and [l]
shorten the vowels, [r] lengthens them.   Among consonants,
spirants are longer than stops, voiceless consonants longer than
voiced, etc.

**Subjective (linguistic) quantity.**   When we speak of quantity
in phonetics, however, we usually understand quite another
thing than these little variations of which we have just given
some examples.   These are automatic and unconscious.   One
needs apparatus and careful measurements to discover them.
They cannot play a linguistic role, properly speaking.   In a
very great number of languages we make use, however, of
differences of quantity in the same way as qualitative differences to distinguish words and forms.   The vowels in English
*seat* and *sit* are felt as different and give two different meanings
to the "s–t" frame.   In the same way, in French *bête* and *bette*,
*reine* and *renne*, there is a quantitative difference between the
vowels (or, at least, there may be one).   In such a case a short
vowel is contrasted with a long vowel just as an [i] is contrasted
with an [ɑ].   Certain languages make great use of quantitative

differences. In Latin the present *vĕnit* (he comes) was distinguished from the perfect *vēnit*[1] (he came) only by means of the quantity of the vowel [e]. The Finno-Ugric languages (Finnish, Lapp, Estonian, etc.) make considerable use of quantitative differences, even in unstressed syllables. In Finnish, *tule* means "come" (imperative), *tulee* "he comes" (present indicative). Estonian possesses three degrees of vocalic length: short, long, very long. The word *sada* (short *a*) means "one hundred," *saada* (long *a*) "send" (imperative), and *saada* (very long *a*) "to have permission to" (infinitive), etc. In the Germanic languages, quantitative vocalic differences are, most often, accompanied by important qualitative differences (English: *beat* : *bit*, *fool* : *full*; German *fühlen* : *füllen*). The short vowels are at the same time more open and more lax.

This type of quantitative difference implies that the "long" phoneme in a given phonetic setting has a duration sufficiently greater than that of the "short" phoneme for the ear to perceive the difference and for the speaker to have a clear impression of the distinction. It is sufficient then that a long [i] be longer than a short [i] before the same consonant. But nothing prevents a "short" [a] from having the same duration, or from being longer than a "long" [i]. Meyer has demonstrated that the English [æ] of *man* is longer (its average duration is 22.4 hundredths of a second) than a "long" [i] (20.1). We shall call this perceived and conscious quantity *subjective quantity* (functional or linguistic quantity). It is to this quantity that one refers when one speaks in linguistics of *shorts* and *longs*.[2]

Certain investigations made recently in the field of phonetic quantity have, however, demonstrated that what we perceive subjectively as a difference of quantity or of length is in reality often something else. A long subjective duration is often accompanied by a falling intonation which, at least in certain cases, is the only difference that can be noted objectively between it and the "short," which is characterized in its turn by a rising or level intonation. The measured duration may be

---

[1] The use of ⌣ and ⁻ to indicate short and long vowels respectively is traditional in Latin linguistics.

[2] Certain modern phoneticians reserve the term "duration" for the measurable quantity, and use "length" for the linguistically functional quantity.

the same for the "longs" and the "shorts." We are indebted
to Marguerite Durand for these remarkable findings, based on
materials drawn from the most diverse languages. But one
must avoid too great a generalization. It is perfectly possible
to combine a long subjective quantity with a rising melody and
vice versa, as the author of these lines believes he has demonstrated with the help of Swedish and Norwegian materials.
The impression of length may also be due to differences of
contact between a vowel and the following consonant. In
English, it is questionable if the quantity as such or the qualitative differences should be regarded as the essential characteristic. If the notion of (subjective) length in phonetics is often
based on other differences than those of duration, it is, on the
other hand, evident that quantitative differences properly
speaking may play a linguistic role and that they often do so.
It seems according to measurements that the "longs" are in
general longer than the "shorts" by about 50 per cent, in cases
where it is a question of true quantitative differences.

Consonants also may be long or short (subjective quantity).
In cases where a consonant is divided into two parts by a
syllabic boundary, we speak of a *geminate* consonant (or
*double* or *long* consonant). A geminate consonant may be
defined as a succession: implosive consonant + explosive
consonant (see p. 68), the two consonants being otherwise
identical. Double consonants are well represented in certain
languages, not so well in others. Italian is rich in double
consonants (*fatto*, *bello*), Spanish has none, nor has English.[3]

It should be noted that double letters in spelling in many
languages have no phonetic value and correspond to simple
consonants in pronunciation (English *collar*, *matter*, *knocking*;
French *aller*, *mettons*, *guerre*). French has a tendency in
modern pronunciation to introduce double consonants in certain scholarly words, under the influence of spelling (*villa*,
*illusion*, *collègue*, *immigration*). French [r] is doubled in the
future and the conditional of the verbs *courir*, *mourir*, and

---

[3] In cases where two successive consonants on morpheme boundaries are
identical and, consequently, a geminate would occur, English (as well as German)
has a tendency to reduce the group (*u[n]known*). As far as Spanish *rr* is
concerned (in *carro* as opposed to *caro*), the difference is felt by native speakers
as one of quality, not of quantity.

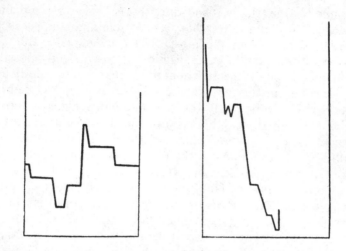

FIG. 51. Melodic curves of the short nasal [ã] of French *content* (LEFT) and of the long nasal [ā] of *contente* (RIGHT). The long vowel is characterized by a markedly falling melody. (According to Marguerite Durand.)

*acquérir* (*courrai, mourrait,* etc.). Apart from these cases, long consonants in French are due either to the dropping of a "feminine" [ə] (*tir(e)rait, nett(e)té, extrêm(e)ment, là-d(e)dans*), or else to the coming together of two words in the sentence (*grande dame, une noix*). One also says: *il l'a dit,* and even often: *je l'ai dit,* with a geminate *l*. French does not have the Germanic tendency to reduce such geminates.

Length may also be used as an *emphatic* or *emotional* means of expression (English *bad!* with a very long vowel, German "*schöön!*"). French uses a long consonant (and not a geminate) to give emphasis to a syllable (*C'est épouvantable!*, with a long *p* which in this case belongs entirely to the syllable following).

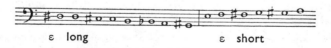

ε long      ε short

FIG. 52. The melody of the long [ɛ] of French *épaisse* (LEFT) and the short [ɛ] of French *épais* (the former falling, the latter slightly rising).

**Syllabic quantity.**  Even syllables may differ in length.  A syllable which contains a long vowel, or a short vowel followed by at least one (long) consonant or by a group of consonants, is called a *long syllable*.  In Latin, a long syllable was equivalent in prosody to two short ones.  The long syllable contained two *morae*, the short one a single mora.  Certain Germanic languages in modern times possess only long syllables.  A syllable contains either a long vowel, or else a short vowel followed by a long consonant (or double consonant) or a group of consonants.  Certain languages (like Finnish) possess four possibilities of combinations: short vowel + short consonant, short vowel + long consonant, long vowel + short consonant, long vowel + long consonant.  (E.g., *tuli* "fire," *tulli* "customs," *tuuli* "wind," *tuulla* "to be windy," in Finnish.)

# CHAPTER IX

# Accents

Certain parts of a sequence of sounds may be emphasized at the expense of others. Most often it is syllables which are thus contrasted with each other by means of certain characteristics which are called *accents* or *prosodic phenomena*. A prosodic contour does not characterize a single phoneme but a succession of phonemes. The phonetic means which are employed to distinguish, one from another, those units which are larger than phonemes (morae, syllables, groups) are also called *prosodemes* or *suprasegmental phonemes*.[1]

The pinpointing of such a unit may be effected by means of intensity, or, more properly speaking, loudness. We then talk about *intensity accent* or, usually with reference to English, *stress* (also *expiratory accent*, if one refers to the articulation, or *dynamic accent*, if reference is made to perceived intensity). The sounds of a stressed syllable are articulated with more force and are consequently more sonorous (more audible) than the others. When emphasis of certain parts of the sentence is carried out with the help of pitch variation, one speaks of *musical accent* or *intonation*. The physical counterpart of pitch is (as was underlined in Chapter I) fundamental frequency (in speech, the frequency of the vocal cords).

**Stress.** In a spoken sentence all the syllables are never produced with the same intensity. Some are weaker (*unstressed*), others stronger (*stressed*). Let us take French and languages with a similar system first. In French, it is always the last syllable of the group which is the strongest and which bears the main stress. A word is usually said to have its stress on such or such a syllable (in French on the last syllable). According to what has been said previously (p. 70) this expression is incorrect. It is not the word (semantic unit) but the group (phonetic unit) which is characterized by such or such an

---

[1] See also Chap. XI.

accentuation.  We have already said that the tendency to make
the word coincide with the phonetic group is much stronger in
certain languages (for example English) than in some other
languages (for example French).  It is true that a word pronounced separately always has a stress, but in such a case the
word is at the same time a group, and it is by virtue of this that
it is stressed.  There are, however, reasons of a practical order
which favor the preservation of the traditional term *word accent*
or *word stress*, although this stress very often disappears when
we combine the word with other words in a sentence (cf. our
French examples above, p. 71).  This reservation once made,
we can safely use the convenient traditional terminology from
now on without being misunderstood.

The rules which determine the place of the stress in words
(groups) vary greatly among different languages.  French
belongs to the languages which are said to have a *fixed stress*,
i.e., the place of the stress is fixed once and for all, and determined automatically by the phonetic structure of the group.
In French, this stress always falls, as we said, on the last
syllable.  This phonetic law is so strong that in pronouncing
foreign words the French will always place the accent on the
last syllable, thus murdering, quite often, the native pronunciation (*Washingtón, Osló, Stockhólm, Mussolini*).  By virtue of the
same tendency, scholarly words borrowed from Latin are often
pronounced in French with a stress quite different from the one
used in Latin (Latin: *técnicus*, French: *technique*, Latin: *legí-
timus*, French: *légitíme*).

In other languages, the location of stress may be fixed in
another manner.  In Finnish and in Czech, the first syllable of
the word always receives the stress, in Polish the last but one.
In Latin, the stress—whatever its phonetic character may have
been—was on the penultimate or the antepenultimate (the
second or the third from the end) according to the quantity of
the penultimate.

These languages, where the stress is fixed by automatic rules,
are very different from languages where the place of the stress
is free, i.e., independent of the phonetic structure as such.  In
such languages it is possible to change the meaning of a word
or a form by changing the place of the stress.  In this case the
place of the stress consequently plays a linguistic role and is a

distinctive phenomenon which conveys meaning. English is a good example of a *free stress* language. If we pronounce *import* with the expiratory accent on the first syllable, it is a substantive ("importation"). If we place the stress on the second syllable, the word is a verb ("to import").[2] In Spanish, *cánto* with the stress on the first syllable means "I sing," while *cantó*, with the stress on the second syllable, means "he sang." The word *término* with the stress on the first syllable means "term" in Spanish, *termíno* with the stress on the second syllable "I terminate," and *terminó* means "he terminated." In Russian, the position of the stress is likewise very free and often changes from one form to another in the paradigm. A word stressed on the last syllable is called an *oxytone*; a word whose accent is on the last syllable but one a *paroxytone*, while when the third syllable from the last is stressed the word is called a *proparoxytone*.

There are also important differences from language to language in the force with which the stressed syllables are pronounced in relation to the unstressed syllables. In French, the difference is very weak, with the result that the unstressed syllables retain all of their articulative precision, while in Germanic languages the stressed syllables may be very strong and the unstressed very weak (cf. p. 59).

Even in languages where the place of the accent is regulated, as in French, it is possible, however, to use stress to express *emphasis* or *emotion*. These types of stress may be called respectively *emphatic* and *emotional* stress. They normally imply an extra stress on a syllable other than the one which normally receives the stress. If a Frenchman says: *C'est épouvantable*, he automatically places the stress on *-tab-*, but if he wishes to express emotion he may also place another stress on *-pou-* (lengthening its consonant at the same time) and thereby oppose, to a simple statement, an affective or emotional expression. In English, we may oppose emphatically *ím-pressionism* to *éxpressionism* by stressing the normally unstressed first syllable (*contrast emphasis*).

---

[2] This is at least true generally for British English pronunciation. Both British and American English use this procedure, though they often disagree on the accentuation of particular words.

**Musical accent.** While stress consists in variations of the sound intensity (or more exactly, since it is a question of perception, loudness), musical accent implies variations in the pitch. We have already seen that individual speakers use many different registers and consequently the actual pitches used in a given utterance will vary considerably from speaker to speaker. But it is not the absolute pitch which is interesting from the linguistic point of view; it is the *relative pitch* and, above all, the variations of pitch and the intervals. In short, it is the *melody* which is significant and which concerns the linguist.

Musical variations in speech are used differently according to language. In most European languages, melody is especially important for the phonetics of the sentence. It is thanks to melodic differences, or *intonation*, that we can express all sorts of mental states or feelings (satisfaction, discontent, surprise, disappointment, contempt, hatred, etc.). In English, in French, and in many other languages, we may change a statement into a question simply by means of intonation. Very often, a language uses the same intonation contour to indicate a question, as opposed to a statement, and to signal something unfinished (the first part of a longer sentence).

In (Brit.) Engl. such a sentence as "If you don't believe me, I can't help it" has the following intonation (Fig. 53; according to Armstrong). The first part ends in a rising manner (tune 2; the type which is normally found in questions), the second in a falling manner (tune 1; the type used in a statement). There are in English, as in French, two principal types which are opposed to each other and which may both be varied *ad infinitum*.

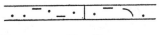

FIG. 53.

In Standard American a sentence like "This is my wife" has (according to Clifford H. Prator) the following intonation pattern (normal statement, *rising—falling*):

[ˈðis iz mai ˈwaif]
FIG. 54.

It is used in simple statements of fact, in commands, and in questions beginning with an interrogative word (*what, who, why,* etc.).

This intonation is opposed to a *rising intonation,* at the end of other questions than those mentioned ("Are you ready?"):

[ɑ:ju ˈredi]
FIG. 55.

and in non-final groups ("He speaks English, Italian, and French"; the last group final, *rising—falling*):

[hi spi:ks ˈiŋgliʃ iˈtæljən ənd ˈfrɛnʧ]
FIG. 56.

We can illustrate the principal types of intonation in French by the following examples (from Coustenoble-Armstrong):

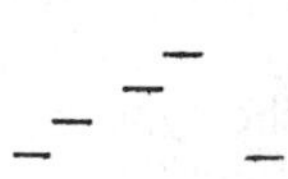

*il est mi-di vingt*
FIG. 57.   (A single group; affirmative tune.)

*il est con·tent?*
FIG. 58.   (A single group; interrogative tune.)

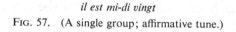

*je n(e) tiens pas à l(e) sa-voir*
FIG. 59.   (Two groups; the first rising, the second falling.)

There are, however, a great number of languages—especially in Africa, in America, and in the Far East—where pitch differences are used to distinguish one word from another. In these languages, tone is a constituent factor of the phonetic structure of the word (or group) and in principle plays the same role as the segmental phonemes[3] of which the word is composed. Chinese gives us a typical example of this. In the Peking dialect there are four *tones* that can be symbolized schematically as follows (according to Karlgren): (1) ⌐ (uniform); (2) / (rising); (3) ∨ (broken); (4) \ (falling). According to the way a group of phonemes like *chu* is pronounced, with one or another of these tones, it means "pork," "bamboo," "lord," or "to dwell, to live." The system of tones in a South African language (Hottentot) is described (by Beach) in the following manner: There are six tones, the first of which is high and rising, the second medium and rising, the third low and rising, the fourth high and falling, the fifth medium and falling, the sixth low and even. In this case, it seems, a combination of the (relative) pitch of the register and the direction of the tonal movement produces six types of tonal contrast which are used with a distinctive function (i.e., to distinguish different words) in this system.

Languages of this type are called *tone languages*. We have seen above that in French, for example, melody can play a similar role, when melodic differences replace the contrast in duration which one subjectively imagines hearing (according to recent researches made by Marguerite Durand; see Figs. 51 and 52, p. 78). It would be going a bit too far, however, to wish to include French, because of this, among tonal languages and to put it on the same footing with Chinese and Hottentot. But it is, on the other hand, a fact that the melodic differences may have a certain distinctive importance even in languages which are not tonal in the proper sense of the word. Among European languages, Lithuanian and Serbo-Croatian are the chief tone languages.

The musical tone of the word has a somewhat different aspect in the two Scandinavian languages which possess tone: Swedish and Norwegian. In these languages, it is necessary for the

3 See Chap. XI.

word (the group) to contain at least two syllables and to have the stress on a syllable other than the last in order to enter into the tonal system. In a monosyllabic or oxytone word there is only one possibility. The languages mentioned possess two musical accents: accent 1 and accent 2. It is by means of the opposition of these two types that we distinguish between words like the Swedish *buren* "the cage" (accent 1) and *buren* "carried" (accent 2), *tanken* "the tank" (accent 1) and *tanken* "the thought" (accent 2), *komma* "comma" (accent 1) and *komma* "to come" (accent 2).[4]   It is difficult to describe these accents in general terms because the form of the melodic curves varies very much from one region to another.   Accent 1, for instance, is clearly falling in certain regions (the Southern part of the country), but more or less rising (in the first syllable)

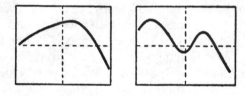

FIG. 60.

in others.   In Fig. 60 we reproduce, as examples, the melodic curves for the two types of accent in the Swedish spoken in Stockholm (words of two syllables).

What is common to all Swedish and Norwegian dialects is not the melody of each type considered as such, but just the existence of two types of tone which are in contrast and by means of which we may distinguish between words and forms.   The accents or prosodemes in question can be defined only in terms of linguistic function, not in terms of frequency variation (melodic curves or tonal patterns).   It is also to be noted that melody is not the only phonetic feature which distinguishes the two Scandinavian accents.   It may be, at the same time, a question of a certain difference of intensity, and perhaps of duration. In words with accent 1, the first syllable is stronger and the second weaker than in accent 2.

---

[4] The spelling does not reflect this difference in pronunciation.

# CHAPTER X

## Experimental Phonetics

The phonetician uses several different methods in his work to examine the sounds of language and their combinations. His most important apparatus is his ear, which will remain his most precious instrument in spite of all the technical inventions of our age. The use of apparatus gives him a better knowledge of the physical phenomena behind the differences perceived, thus completing the testimony of the ear. *Experimental phonetics—*or *instrumental phonetics—*gives us information about physical facts, acoustic and physiological, whereas the auditory analysis informs us about the reactions of our hearing mechanism and of the psychological processes involved in perception.

**Acoustical instruments.** In the chapter on acoustics we have already spoken of the different technical means available today for the acoustical analysis of the sounds of language. Fifty years ago, in the field of acoustics, phoneticians had at their disposal only very modest resources: *tuning forks* and *resonators* to determine the proper tone of the oral cavities, and crude mechanical recordings of vibrations, which were analysed according to Fourier's theorem. Despite this imperfection of the instruments, an astonishingly exact knowledge of the structure of vowels had already been arrived at towards the end of the last century, thanks to the genius of a few great physicists and phoneticians (Helmholtz, Hermann, Rousselot, Pipping). It is, however, only with modern electro-acoustics that we have succeeded in going farther than the phoneticians of the last century. Thanks to the microphone, the cathode oscillograph, filters, and the different acoustic spectrometers, to "visible speech," and to synthetic speech, there is no longer anything, from a technical point of view, to prevent a complete and integral analysis of all details of the sounds used in human language. The oscillograph first permitted a visual recording of sound vibrations (cf. Fig. 9, p. 11), thereby marking the

87

88 PHONETICS

beginning of the modern epoch of acoustic phonetics. It has recently been supplemented by sound film, by filters, by spectrography, and by speech synthesis.

**Physiological instruments.** Among the different means employed to register the various phases of articulation, the kymograph was for a long time the most important apparatus; and it is undeniable that it still renders the phonetician many services despite the invention of more efficient new methods.

Thanks to the kymograph cylinder, it is possible to register the different articulatory movements—of the tongue, lips, soft palate, and breath—on blackened paper and thus obtain a graph that can be easily analyzed. With the help of Marey's capsule and a rubber membrane, it is also possible, by speaking into a mouth-piece, to obtain a graph showing fluctuations in the air stream, thus making it possible to establish the physiological difference between a vowel, a spirant and a stop, as far as the air stream is concerned. The same graph also indicates the presence or absence of vibrations of the vocal cords. With the aid of a special nasal curve we can study the importance of nasalization. The tracings obtained with the kymograph, called *kymograms*, are thus graphs of articulation which in principle cannot be compared with the acoustic graphs obtained by an electrical sound wave recording. However, it is also possible, by means of a microphone and a special mechanism (called a "Kettererschreiber" in German), to reproduce sound vibrations from a microphone, a gramophone, or a tape recorder on the blackened paper of the cylinder. In this case we will be dealing with an acoustic graph, though one much less accurate than that obtained by means of electronic devices.

On the physiological kymogram it is possible to study not only the different articulatory qualities of sounds but also the quantitative (time) and musical facts (vocal cord frequency). The duration of each phase of articulation can be measured on the graph. Provided that the laryngeal vibrations are recorded, the variations in the frequency of the glottal tone can be calculated by measuring the length of the periods on the kymograms and by constructing from this a logarithmic graph of the variations of frequency. The lower the tone, the greater is the length of the periods, and inversely.   In principle it is by such a process that the melodic curves reproduced in Fig. 60 have been obtained.

Only with difficulty can variations of intensity be determined from the kymogram.   The amplitude obtained on the tracing is not only a function of the amplitude of the sound vibration emitted but is also influenced by phenomena of resonance—the closer the natural vibration of the recording body to the recorded tone, the greater the amplitude will be (cf. p. 10)— and by the varying and often considerable inertia of the mechanisms employed.   We must have recourse to an oscillographic recording in order to measure the amplitude of the

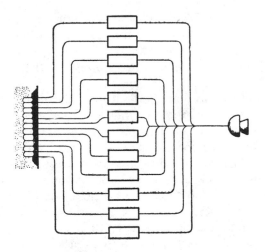

FIG. 61.   Schematic sketch of the filters of the sound spectrograph as used in *Visible Speech*.   From the microphone (RIGHT) the sound passes into the different filters (twelve in number, each of 300 c/s).   Each filter lets pass through only those frequencies—of the many contained in the complex wave—falling within its domain.   When the sound becomes visible on the screen (LEFT), there is no longer a single complex wave but a series of frequencies arranged from low to high according to their rate of vibration.   This is the sound spectrum.

vibrations (one of the physical factors behind the linguistic concept of stress).   Another method of registering articulation in addition to the kymographic method is *palatography*. Palatograms are obtained by means of an *artificial palate* placed in the mouth of the subject being examined.   After the latter has pronounced the desired sound or group of sounds he removes the artificial palate, and it can be seen immediately what parts have been touched by the tongue. The place of articulation and the degree of raising of the tongue in the mouth are thus determined. It goes without saying that sounds articulated in the back part of the mouth are difficult to study by means of palatography. Labial and nasal articulations are not seen in it at all. Recently a photographic process has begun to replace the artificial palate. The subject's own palate is dyed, and after the required sound has been articulated the palate is photographed directly—which obviously allows for a more normal and natural articulation.

Palatography is supplemented, or replaced, in modern phonetics by X-rays, which allow us to study the position of all the organs of speech at any point during articulation or—thanks to X-ray motion pictures—the movements of these organs during the pronunciation of whole phrases. If these films are combined with a sound recording, we can at the same time listen to the sounds produced and look at the movements executed by the organs to achieve these sounds. This is one of the most valuable inventions of modern physiological phonetics.

Starting from the spectrograms obtained by the Sonagraph and similar machines it is now possible to reconstruct synthetic spectrograms and have them transformed into sound. In this way it has become possible to vary deliberately any phonetic factor, leaving all the rest unaltered, and thereby examine its role in the communication process. It is, for example, possible to examine whether, in a system of word accent contrasts, pitch is the most important factor, or if other phenomena contribute to, or are alone responsible for the linguistic phenomenon perceived.

# CHAPTER XI

# Phonemics or "Functional Phonetics"

**Functional and nonfunctional factors.** It follows from what has been said above that the number of sounds, even within a single language, is almost unlimited. We do not pronounce a vowel or even a consonant twice consecutively in exactly the same way. The context of a given sound differs from one case to another, causing a wide range of variation. The accentuation, rate of delivery, pitch, and the qualities of the voice vary from one occasion to the other and from individual to individual. There are differences of pronunciation between individuals which are due to anatomical differences or to individual habits. Spectrograms reveal important differences between vowels of men and those of women and small children. These differences do not impede comprehension. They are not perceived by the speakers. People *think* they pronounce and hear the same thing despite these variations, which are sometimes considerable.

We may therefore with justice ask ourselves why, despite all these combinatory or individual differences, we identify the vowels and consonants of other speakers with our own. Why do we identify a woman's [i] with a man's, or the [ɑ] after [l] with an [ɑ] after [s] or [t]? And why does a Frenchman believe he hears the same initial consonant in *qui* and *coup*, in *tas* and *tôt* when the phonetic analysis has proved the existence of considerable differences? Spectrograms show acoustically different units which, nevertheless, may be identified by the listener as one and the same. Palatograms and X-rays show equally considerable differences in articulation. And finally, why does a Frenchman from Paris, who pronounces a back *r*, immediately identify a word like *rire*, pronounced by a Southern Frenchman who rolls his *r*'s with the tip of his tongue? The answer is that the [k] before [i] and the [k] before [u], the "masculine" [i] and the "feminine" [i], the [ɑ] after [s] and the [ɑ] after [l], the rolled *r* and the uvular *r* are identical from the viewpoint of their *linguistic function*. Certain characteristics of the sounds of language are important for identification, certain others are not. Each vowel and each consonant articulated in a context contain *distinctive* or *relevant* features alongside a number of *nondistinctive* or *nonrelevant* ones.

Actually, if we had at our disposal an unlimited number of infinitely variable units, no organized communication would be possible by means of these units. A system of communication such as language necessarily presupposes a *limited* number of elements and a *restricted* number of features that distinguish these elements from one another. The fundamental difference between a linguistic expression and a nonlinguistic expression (for example a cry of pain) is that the former may be broken down into smaller units, units which recur farther on in the spoken chain, combined in a different way (at least if the expression is sufficiently extended). Such units are called *discrete*.[1] The cry of pain, on the other hand, is a complex of nondiscrete elements.

Let us take as an example a phrase such as *The city of London is wonderful*. If you ask an English-speaking person who is not a phonetician to group together the sound units which seem to him identical in this sentence, there is no doubt that he will identify the two [i]'s of *city* with that of *is*, the [ʌ] of *London* with that of *wonderful*, and the initial [l] of *London* with the final one of *wonderful*, in spite of the differences which exist between these units from a purely phonetic point of view. In British pronunciation there is, for example, a very audible difference between the "clear" *l* of *London* and the "dark" *l* of *wonderful*. In this latter case it is hardly a question of differences too subtle for the human ear. But in English the distinction between the two *l*'s is not used as distinctive in the system. It is a nonrelevant feature. Consequently the Englishman is not accustomed to attaching importance to the difference which exists between these two consonantal qualities. He cannot change the meaning of a word by replacing a "clear" *l* by a "dark" *l*, or vice versa. The difference is not *functional*

---

[1] That they are called "discrete" (with a term borrowed from mathematics) implies that there is no gradual passage from one to the other but that they are sharply delimited from each other. A linguistic unit is *either* A *or* B.

(distinctive).   Both *l*'s are *variants*, or *allophones* of the same phoneme.

**Phonemes.**   The concept of *phoneme*, in the sense explained here, is relatively recent in linguistics and phonetics, and has been defined in several different ways.   But the distinction between, on the one hand, the innumerable concrete sounds and, on the other, the functional units (conceived as types or classes of sounds) has been perceived more or less clearly and consciously by all the scientists who have occupied themselves with problems of phonetics (the Frenchmen Passy, Meillet, Grammont; the Dane Jespersen, the Swede Noreen, etc., and, later, the famous British phonetician Daniel Jones).   It would take too long to relate here the different attempts made by modern linguists to define the phoneme.[2]   We prefer to give a few more examples which, we believe, will illustrate, better than theoretical considerations, the essential difference between phonemes and variants (allophones).

The two types of *r* (anterior and posterior) are variants of the same phoneme in French.   Since the choice of one or the other of the two types is not determined by the surroundings of the word (but by individual or regional habits), we speak in this case of *free variants*.   The palatal [k] (of *qui*) and the velar [k] (of *coup*) are also variants of a single phoneme /k/,[3] but since, in this case, the choice is automatically determined by the vocalic context, we speak here of *combinatory variants*.   The nasals, liquids, and "semi-vowels" unvoiced in contact with voiceless consonants in French are also examples of combinatory variants (in *pneu, pli, puis, pied*, etc.).

**Contrast (opposition).**   We say of two phonemes that they are in *contrast* or *opposition*.[4]   Thus there is opposition in

[2] There are profound differences in the manner of defining a phoneme among linguists like Jones, Trubetzkoy, Hjelmslev, and Bloomfield, according to their conception of language.   For these problems, which depend on linguistic theory, see Perrot, *La linguistique*, pp. 110 *et seq.*   American readers are particularly referred to Bloomfield, *Language*, Twaddell, *On Defining the Phoneme*, and Harris, *Methods in Structural Linguistics*.

[3] / / is used to indicate phonemes; [ ] indicates allophones, or sounds without consideration of their linguistic function.

[4] It may seem convenient to distinguish between "contrast" and "opposition," the former referring to the distinctions within the chain of phonemes

English between [r] and [l], [p] and [b], [t] and [d], [i] and [u], etc., since it is possible to change the meaning of a word by replacing one with the other (*right*:*light*, *pair*:*bare*, *town*:*down*, *fit*:*foot*, etc.). In the same way in French (*rit*:*lit*, *peau*:*beau*, etc.). French has another opposition which is not found in English: [i]:[y] (in French *lit* [li]:*lu* [ly], *vie* [vi]:*vue* [vy], etc.). But there is no contrast in French between front *r* and back *r*, nor between voiced [l] and voiceless [l̥],[5] as is the case, for example, in Welsh (where the *ll* of the spelling represents a voiceless lateral phoneme opposed to voiced *l*; cf. Welsh names like *Lloyd*). It may happen that two sounds which are in contrast with each other in certain phonetic positions are not contrasted in certain others. The two vowels [e] and [ε] are contrasted in French in stressed open syllables (*dé*:*dais*, *fée*: *fait*). But before a consonant in the same syllable the opposition is no longer possible. A Frenchman always pronounces an open [ε] (*fer*, *ciel*, *net*, *verre*, *même*, etc.). The closed [e] does not exist before a consonant of the same syllable in French. We say that, in this position, the opposition [e]:[ε] is *neutralized* (or that there is *syncretism*). It is by virtue of this phonetic law that an [e] changes automatically into [ε] if it happens to find itself in a closed syllable (*céder* [sede] but *je cède* [sεd]).

All languages do not use either the same number of oppositions, nor the same types. French makes use, as we have said, of two series of palatal (oral) vowels: a rounded series [y], [ø], and [œ] and a nonrounded series [i], [e], and [ε]. Neither Italian nor Spanish possesses rounded front vowels (nor does English). Labialization is therefore not used in these systems as a means of distinction, and Italians and Spaniards, in speaking French, often have much difficulty distinguishing between *si* and *su*, *fée* and *feu*, *mère* and *meurt*. On the other hand, English has central vowels unknown in French, Italian, and Spanish. Nor does Spanish, for example, possess the distinction between half-close and half-open vowels (French or Italian [e] and [ε], [o] and [ɔ]). The differences in closing which unquestionably occur in the pronunciation of the different

---

(*the syntagm*), the latter to the distinctions in the system (*the paradigm*). This terminology, however, has not been applied with any rigor in this book.

[5] A [ ̥ ] in phonetic script indicates voicelessness.

Spanish *e*'s and *o*'s are of a combinatory nature, determined
by the context and consequently not perceived by the subjects
speaking.   The distinction [e]:[ɛ] is not relevant in Spanish
and the two vocalic qualities are two combinatory variants, or
allophones, of the same phoneme.

Italian, like French, contrasts a close [e] with an open [ɛ] and
a close [o] with an open [ɔ] (cf. *téma* "fear," and *tèma*, "theme";
*rócca* "spinning wheel," and *ròcca* "rock").   Consequently,
Spanish and Italian possess the same number of vowel sounds
(or vocalic timbres) but the Italian system is richer in vowel
phonemes than the Spanish system.   The vowels of Italian can
be arranged diagrammatically as follows:

i                     u

e          o

ɛ      ɔ

a

FIG. 62.

This is at the same time the chart of vowel *phonemes*.   The
same chart also holds good for Spanish if we consider only the
principal phonetic vowel *sounds* which exist in this language.[6]
But if we wish to represent the system of Spanish vowel *phonemes* (its possibilities of vowel contrasts), the chart would have
the following appearance:

i          u

e      o

a

FIG. 63.

In English and in French, /s/ and /z/ (voiceless and voiced
sibilants) are two separate phonemes.   We can distinguish
between English *peace* and *peas*, French *baisser* and *baiser*, or
between *chausse* and *chose*, solely through the distinction

[6] There are in Spanish, as in Italian, other vocalic nuances of a combinative
nature which we do not take into account here.

between /s/ and /z/. Spanish, too, has these two sounds phonetically, but only as variants of the same phoneme, since the phoneme /s/ is automatically pronounced as a voiced consonant before another voiced consonant (*mismo*), and as a voiceless one in all other positions (*casa, mes*). Spanish thus possesses the same phonetic difference as French between [s] and [z] but does not use it in its functional system. There is no /s/:/z/ opposition in Spanish.

Spanish possesses a series of voiced stops ([b], [d], [g]) alongside which there exists a series of voiced fricatives having the same point of articulation. But these spirants (transcribed [β], [ð], [ɤ]) are only variants of the phonemes /b/, /d/, /g/. Spanish uses one or the other (stop or spirant) depending on whether the phonemes occur in strong or weak position in the spoken chain. Spanish cannot, for example, oppose a [d] stop to the corresponding spirant [ð] (as does English in *day*:*they*). The phonetic difference *voiced stop*:*voiced spirant* is not distinctive, or relevant, in Spanish.

Swedish offers us a good example of a language in which a melodic difference is used to distinguish one word from another (cf. p. 85). The tone or musical accent is therefore, in this language, a pertinent feature of the phonetic structure of the word. It is a phoneme or, since in this case it is a question of a musical phenomenon, a *toneme*. The different tones of Chinese also are tonemes. In language systems where duration is used as a means of distinction (Latin *vĕnit*:*vēnit*; French *bête*:*bette*; cf. p. 75), we sometimes talk about a *chroneme* (Jones).

Functional phonetics also has a quantitative aspect. The *frequency of occurrence* and the *distribution* of phonemic units in the utterance is another question of structure. *Phonemic statistics* is becoming an important branch of phonetics. For phonemic structure is not only a question of possible distinctions but also of how, and to what extent, the possibilities are utilized in the different sequences which build up the utterance (syllables, words, periods, etc.). There are important differences between languages in this respect, too.

These examples will suffice to show that a *functional* or *structural* analysis must necessarily supplement the physical analysis of sounds and articulations. If we limit ourselves to establishing that Spanish has, like French, two kinds of *s* (voiced and voiceless) or, like English, a [d] stop and a corresponding fricative [ð], without troubling ourselves about the fact that these phonetic differences function differently from one language to the other, we are neglecting an important aspect of the phonetic peculiarities of the languages in question. Traditional phonetics neglected this analysis and therefore provided an *incomplete description* of the linguistic expression.

**Phonemics (phonology).** The study which sets out to determine the phonetic distinctions which, in a given language, have a differential value, and to establish the system of phonemes and prosodemes is called *phonemics*, or *phonology*. Taken in this sense, phonology was founded at Prague about thirty-five years ago by a group of linguists (Trubetzkoy, Jakobson, and others), whence the name *Prague School*. A similar development took place in the United States (Sapir, Bloomfield, etc.), perhaps independently of the European movement. Since the name *phonology*, proposed by the Prague group, has also been used in other senses (by Grammont to mean general acoustical and physiological phonetics; by others to mean "phonetics" quite simply), most linguists nowadays prefer the term *phonemics*, a term which is almost general in America and is beginning to be more and more frequent also in Europe.

**Phonetics and phonemics.** Phonetics proper, as described in the preceding chapters, and phonemics, whose general principles we have just briefly outlined, are not two autonomous and independent sciences. It was a grave error on the part of the Prague School to want to establish a strict separation between phonetics—a natural science which makes use of instrumental means—and phonology—a linguistic science. The study of the acoustical and physiological facts of human speech should be pursued parallel to the study of the function of the different units and of the structure of the system used in speaking. Phonemics establishes the number of contrasts utilized and their mutual relationships. Experimental phonetics determines, with its different methods, the physical and physiological nature of the distinctions established. Without linguistic analysis of systems and functional units, the experimenter would not know what to do.   And without the physical and physiological analysis of all the facts of pronunciation, the linguist would not know the physical nature of the contrasts established.   The two types of studies are interdependent and condition each other.   Consequently it seems preferable to group them together under the traditional general heading of *phonetics*.

# CHAPTER XII
# Evolutionary Phonetics

**Phonetic change.** It is a well-known fact that the pronunciation of a language does not always remain the same. In the course of its history it undergoes numerous changes, sometimes slow, sometimes rather rapid. The simple fact—already pointed out in this work—that spelling does not always correspond with pronunciation proves that the latter was formerly different from what it is now. The pronunciation has changed but the old spelling has remained.[1] Written language is more conservative than spoken language.

When it comes to answering the question why pronunciation changes, the scholar finds himself facing almost insurmountable difficulties. Sounds are not the only things that change in a language. Forms, syntax, vocabulary, and literary style also change. It would be going too far beyond the limits of this little book to take up the problem of linguistic change in its entirety. This change, moreover, is probably only a particular aspect of a more general problem—that of change in all aspects of life—social, political, and cultural, and changes in all the rules which together determine the relationships between men. Human language is a social fact, and the changes undergone by the linguistic habits of a group can be explained only within the framework of the transformations of society in general. It would be erroneous to want to isolate a language from its milieu, without which it cannot be understood, and whose stable characteristics as well as transformations it reflects. We shall have to limit ourselves here to a rapid and necessarily brief analysis of a few of the factors which contribute to determine the result of phonetic changes.

[1] This is not the only explanation of the lack of correspondence between spelling and pronunciation. French and English spelling, for example, still retains many traces of the etymological preoccupations of the grammarians of the Renaissance. It must also be remembered that our alphabet—inherited from the Romans—is ill adapted to rendering the phonemes of many modern languages.

**The role of combinatory phonetics.** We have given some examples of phonetic changes which have occurred during the history of different European languages and which are explained in part by phenomena of combinatory phonetics (assimilation, dissimilation, differentiation, ease of pronunciation, etc.). It is undeniable that these are factors that are constantly at work in a language and that they are creating slight changes in pronunciation everywhere and at all times. Some of these changes are ephemeral; others become stable and form part of the norm. For a long time the role of assimilation in the phonetic history of languages has been particularly stressed. And it is certain that a great number of phenomena of historical phonetics are due to an assimilatory tendency. We also have seen that language often reacts against the unfortunate effects of assimilation, by certain tendencies (differentiation, dissimilation). Metathesis and inversion often result in syllables that are more consistent with the syllabic structure of the language. Parasitic consonants (in Greek *andrós*, French *viendrai*) gives us another example of a phonetic innovation which has its origin in a combinatory phenomenon (cf. p. 60).

**Grammont's general rules.** In his *Traité de phonétique* the French phonetician Maurice Grammont has formulated rules according to which these different phenomena of combinatory phonetics are produced, rules which the author looks upon as rather general in all languages. He has also formulated the famous "law of the stronger," according to which, when two phonemes influence each other in one way or another, it is the weaker (by its position in the syllable or by its own articulatory strength) which is influenced by the other. If, in the French word *jusque* [ʒysk], changed to [ʒyʃk], the [s] has been assimilated to a shibilant consonant (and not the reverse), this is because [s] in this case is implosive (is at the end of a syllable) and consequently weaker than the initial consonant.

In recent years, certain scholars have pointed to the frequency of occurrence of phonemes and of phoneme clusters as a factor in phonetic change. Frequent phonemes are more easily preserved than rare ones, and frequent clusters resist simplification and weakening more easily than less frequent groups. Rare clusters tend to be replaced by more frequent ones, abnormal syllabic types by more current ones, etc.   High frequency of occurrence, of single units and of patterns, may consequently be supposed to be a factor of stability in language.

**Phonetic laws.**  For a long time it was axiomatic among linguists to believe that changes in the sounds of language take place by virtue of *laws* which operate blindly—the supposed *phonetic laws*.  According to this point of view, the same phoneme, in a given phonetic context, in the same language and during a certain period, undergoes the same change in all the words of the language in question.  If for instance the Latin a, in a stressed open syllable, changes to *e* throughout the North of the Gallo-Roman region (the "langue d'oil"), this change must necessarily take place in all Latin words that have been retained in French.  No exceptions to the phonetic laws were accepted other than those which were due to the influence of *analogy*.  The thesis of the absolute character of the phonetic laws was formulated for the first time by the German linguist Leskien (1876).  The so-called *neo-grammarians* especially have defended this thesis and have also lent weight to the idea of the superiority of the *historic method* in linguistics.  Their most famous representative was the German Hermann Paul.

A later generation has, however, strongly modified the neo-grammarian doctrine.  In a study published as early as 1896, the Swedish linguist Axel Kock called attention to a whole series of factors which reduce the action of the phonetic laws.  All words do not have the same frequency in a language—a fact which entails differences of phonetic treatment.  A frequently used, everyday word undergoes the effects of a phonetic tendency more easily than a rarely used, literary or special word.  It is a well-known fact that the various grammatical tools, which are almost always unstressed (articles, pronouns, conjunctions, prepositions), are subject to a much stronger phonetic reduction than the "full" words.  A long Latin *o* in a stressed open syllable tended to become *eu* (originally a diphthong) in French (Latin *flore(m)*, French *fleur*; Latin *dolore(m)*, French *douleur*, etc.).  But in the personal pronouns *nous* and *vous* (whose vowel also goes back to a long Latin *o* and, according to the phonetic law in question, should also have become *eu*), we are dealing with a different phonetic treatment, which is explained in this case by the fact that these words are most often used as atonics before the verb and that as a result they have had a different development. In a French work like *avocat* ("lawyer"), the final α goes back to a Latin α in an open stressed syllable (*advocatus*) which should have become *e* in French. The form of the word is explained in this case, as in hundreds of others, by the learned character of the term. The word did not live in the mouth of the people across centuries of time, but was borrowed at a recent period from Latin, the language of administration and jurisprudence. On the other hand, we are dealing with the normal phonetic representative of the Latin *advocatus* in the French *avoué*. French is rich in *phonetic doublets* of this sort (*hôtel:hôpital*, *rançon:rédemption*), many of which have been taken over by English (*hotel:hospital*, *ransom:redemption*). Certain other exceptions to the phonetic laws are explained by the emotional or emphatic nature of the term in question.

Nowadays, we speak of *phonetic tendency* rather than of *law*. Each phonetic system is dominated by certain articulatory and structural tendencies. These tendencies hold in the majority of cases, while certain words, for various reasons, escape the action of the tendencies in question. A new tendency may prevail in the language of the people or in dialects, but may be thwarted in the upper classes by the influence of the norm. On the other hand, an innovation may be accepted by the upper classes of large cities as a fashion which spreads, but may be ignored among the people or in the country where the normative urban influence no longer makes itself felt, or is less strong. This is for instance the case of the back *r* in a large number of European languages (see p. 46).

Every phonetic innovation has its origin in a particular place and probably with a single individual. But it takes on a linguistic character only at the moment when it becomes common to a whole group. An individual fact of pronunciation is a possible point of departure for a phonetic innovation but does not in itself constitute a linguistic change. For reasons which have yet to be determined but which are doubtless social in character, the innovation spreads from its place of origin, which thus becomes a *center of diffusion*. The farther it goes from this center, the weaker the effect of the tendency becomes. The strength and speed of its spread depend on the prestige of the innovating groups and on the facilities of communication. This is the reason why isolated regions—in mountainous areas, for example—are linguistically conservative, while large cities and regions of intensive farming are innovative. On the periphery of a linguistic area, there are often only a few words that are touched by change. In the same dialect we find words modified by the phonetic tendency, and others which, for one reason or another, have resisted transformation. In reality each word has its own phonetic history. The term "law" is therefore incorrect. Phonetic changes are due to the action of certain tendencies and not to laws in the strict sense of the term.

**Linguistic geography.** It is to *linguistic geography* (or *dialect geography*) that we owe these new discoveries in the field of evolutionary phonetics. Linguistic geography was founded by the German Wenker, and developed particularly by the Swiss Gilliéron, one of the founders of the famous *Atlas linguistique de la France*. Later atlases for other linguistic areas (Germany, Italy, England, the United States, etc.) are modeled on this pioneer work. On the maps of linguistic atlases, the phonetician can study the spread of each word, as well as the different phonetic forms of the same word, and thus trace the limits of their spread. The state of the language of a given place (village, city, or province) is never the result of an absolutely uninterrupted and autochthonous development. Every dialect and every language undergo the influence of other tongues, and these influences depend in their turn on political and cultural currents, which change during the course of the centuries. While formerly the different French patois used to be influenced particularly by the provincial cente˙s (political or ecclesiastical), at the present time they are influenced above all by the language of Paris. While French as well as British English pronunciation has long been, and still is, under the strong influence of a generally accepted norm, German and Italian give examples of languages with a rich phonetic variation and many regional differences even in the pronunciation of the highest social classes. For well-known historical reasons, these areas have had numerous centers of diffusion and have consequently numerous local norms. Only in most recent times is there a tendency towards more uniformity of pronunciation in both German and Italian. If there are also several American English standards of pronunciation the reason for this is primarily historical and social, not linguistic properly speaking. As a matter of fact, phonetic evolution is much more complicated, and the study of historical phonetics much more difficult than the neo-grammarians believed.

**Evolutionary phonetics and the system.** In the traditional studies of historical phonetics, there was a tendency to study the history of each phoneme separately. Phoneticians used to follow, from Latin to French or from Proto-Germanic to modern German, the evolution undergone by a single sound, or a single group of sounds. They would record that the short Latin *o* of a stressed open syllable had first become the diphthong *uo* (a stage preserved by Italian: Latin *focu(m)*, Italian *fuoco*) and then *ue* (the stage in Spanish: *fuego*), finally ending in French as *eu* (French *feu*). Then they tried to explain by articulatory phonetics how these transformations could have come about. But they neglected to take into consideration the fact that at each stage of the evolution (Vulgar Latin, Gallo-Roman, Old French, Modern French), the vowel or diphthong in question had formed part of a vocalic system and that their main concern should be the development of the whole system. When a language changes, it is a question not of isolated sounds that are replaced by other isolated sounds, but of an entire system that is transformed and replaced by another system of a different structure. If the phonetic evolution of a language takes a certain direction and not another which is equally possible from a purely phonetic point of view, this is often because of the influence of the system. No sound evolves independently of the other sounds of the same system. In a phonetic system everything is interdependent.

It is not improbable that the application of the structural point of view in historical phonetics may in many cases be able to help us answer a question which, up to now, has most often remained unanswered—why this or that change takes place in the one case but not in the other. For combinatory phonetics can inform us only about the *possibilities* of evolution.

Grammont's rules—however correct they may be—can at most tell us what the result will be if, in a given group, there is assimilation or dissimilation. But they do not tell why the same group evolves in one particular language, or at a certain period of history, but remains unaltered in another language or during another period of evolution of the same language. Thanks to a more strict application of structural viewpoints, modern diachronic phonetics has better chances to explain the sound changes than the "pre-structural" scholars. André Martinet has laid a solid basis for this kind of research with his idea of the "economy" of phonetic systems.

**The substratum.** In order to explain phonetic evolution, recourse has often been had to the influence of a *substratum*, a term which signifies that a population which takes over a new language keeps its old articulatory habits in pronouncing the sounds of the imported language. For example it has been claimed that a certain number of French phonetic phenomena can be explained in terms of a Gallic substratum. French, according to this theory, is Latin pronounced with a Celtic articulatory base. It is in this way that certain scholars have tried to explain the passage from the Latin *u* (pronounced [u]) to [y] in French and likewise the palatalizing tendency which dominates almost all of the phonetic evolution of French from Latin right up to modern times. In some parts of South America (for instance in Paraguay) we find a form of Spanish pronounced with Indian phonetic habits. Many Belgians speak French on a Germanic (Flemish) substratum.

It is beyond doubt that the substratum can in many cases explain the changes undergone by a language at a certain epoch or in a certain region. And many well-known scholars (Ascoli, Brøndal, van Ginneken, Fouché) have strongly insisted on the importance of this factor in phonetic evolution. But linguists have sometimes gone rather too far in this kind of explanation. It is important to emphasize that the influence exerted by a substratum is not a biological fact. It is not a question of race, as some linguists have maintained. It is quite simply a question of the preservation of a certain articulatory *tradition* in spite of the adoption of a new language. The problem, therefore, has a *social* aspect. There is influence of the substratum in cases where the indigenous population has a sufficiently great social and cultural prestige for its articulatory habits not to have been judged vulgar. This is the case in Paraguay (for quite special historical reasons). But it is not the case in many other regions of Latin America where the number of natives was relatively larger, but where Spanish does not show the least trace of foreign influences. The Indian "accent" was judged vulgar and quickly disappeared from among the upper classes.[2]

When a language undergoes, for a certain time, the phonetic influence of a conquering people (or one of a higher culture), we speak of a *superstratum*. Certain facts of French phonetics, for example, have been "explained" in terms of the Germanic superstratum (under the Frankish kings). The Swiss Romanist W. von Wartburg has especially defended this thesis. On the subject of the superstratum, it is important to make the same observation that we have just made with the substratum. It is necessary to know the social and cultural situation of the region and of the period thoroughly in order to judge the possibility of such an influence. As long as we do not have this knowledge, it is better to be cautious in our conclusions.

Finally, the influence exerted on a language by a neighboring language may be called an *adstratum*. For instance, the French spoken in Alsace shows many traces of Germanic phonetics. The Swedish dialect spoken in Finland is strongly influenced, from a phonetic point of view, by Finnish, etc.

It results from what has been said that neither phonetics nor linguistics by itself is capable of explaining phonetic changes. It is necessary to go beyond the limits of phonetics—and even those of linguistics—in order to find, if possible, all the factors which together determine the evolution of sounds—and that of languages.

[2] The author of these lines has studied such problems in a work entitled *L'espagnol dans le Nouveau Monde—problème de linguistique générale* (Lund, 1948).

## CHAPTER XIII

# Importance and Practical Applications of Phonetics

It would in reality be contrary to the very spirit of science to argue about the utility of the various kinds of scientific research. The usefulness—the practical application—of a discovery is a secondary consequence of it and can never be its aim. The scientist works in order to deepen his knowledge of nature and of man. Those scientific results whose usefulness has been the greatest, in physics or in medicine, have often been obtained without the least utilitarian consideration in mind. The practical application has often been an unexpected consequence of researches done solely to satisfy the scientist's curiosity.

If we have nevertheless devoted a few pages at the end of this volume to discussing possible practical applications of phonetics, this is not done to justify or to defend a discipline which, like every other, is, and ought to be, an end in itself. The phonetician works in order to understand better the spoken language. But since this volume is aimed primarily at a public of nonspecialists and students, it is fitting to call attention to a few areas where we have the right to expect from our phonetic researches some "useful" results and some practical applications.

Since phonetics is a branch of linguistics, it is evident, first of all, that it is of considerable importance for the other fields of language study. The study of the history of languages necessarily presupposes a good orientation in matters of descriptive and evolutionary phonetics. To the dialect geographer phonetics is indispensable. And in the field of linguistic theory, phonetics has been of capital importance. The structural concept—which is daily gaining ground among linguists and which consists of regarding language as a system and not as an agglomeration of heterogeneous bodies—was applied first (thanks to phonology; cf. p. 97) to the study of the sounds of language. And in a general way more progress has been made, from the methodological point of view, in the structural description of sounds than in the fields of grammar and of semantics (the *content* of language), where we are now more and more trying to profit from methodical experiments done during the course of analysis of linguistic *expression*. But this is still an example of the purely scientific interest of phonetics.

**The teaching of diction.** At the present time spoken language has assumed an importance formerly unknown. Thanks to such inventions as the telephone, radio, phonograph, loudspeaker, tape recorder, and the sound film, spoken language is more and more replacing written language. One must know how to speak and to speak well, in order to reach one's public and gain the influence which one desires. The way one pronounces is no longer the private affair of the speaker, but something which concerns all those who listen to the speeches of politicians, scientists, artists, and official representatives of society. The public is no longer, as formerly, a small group of relatives, friends, or neighbors assembled within a radius of at most a few yards of the person speaking. His hearers may number thousands or even millions.

*Diction*, the art of pronouncing well, has assumed an important place in modern teaching and doubtless will merit even greater attention. Phonetics is the necessary base of all teaching of this kind. One must understand the mechanism of breathing and the functioning of the glottis in order to teach pupils a proper phonation. Poor breathing and a hoarse voice annoy the listener and tire the person who is speaking. Many a young teacher has found that he cannot teach efficiently because, to his own amazement, he cannot speak efficiently! It is necessary to know thoroughly the articulatory work of the tongue, lips, and soft palate, etc., in order to be able to correct the errors of pronunciation of all kinds which we encounter among a large number of persons—children and adults. In principle *phoniatrics* concerns itself with all the pathological phenomena of pronunciation, whether these be of an articulatory character (due to anatomical imperfections or to bad habits), or whether they are caused by disorders of the central nervous system (phenomena of *aphasia*), or by imperfect hearing. But the treatment of pathological phonetic phenomena necessarily supposes a knowledge of normal phonetics. The person wishing to correct an abnormal [s] in a pupil will be able to achieve this only if he knows the physical and physiological characteristics of a normal [s]. Phoniatrics is only a particular aspect of phonetics, namely the application of the latter to the treatment of the imperfections and maladies of articulated language.

**Pronunciation of foreign languages.** The teaching of foreign languages is also a field in which phonetics has a very great practical importance. Anyone wishing to learn to pronounce a foreign language properly will first have to acquire the mastery of a large number of new articulatory habits (a new articulatory basis; see p. 71). He must accustom himself to articulate the foreign sounds exactly as native speakers do in the language in question, and not to continue using habits peculiar to his native language. We should not think that it is just a matter of learning a few strange new sounds and otherwise making do with sounds already known from our own language. In fact, a whole system of articulatory habits, including intonation and other prosodic phenomena, has to be replaced by something new. Without a thorough knowledge of the phonetics of the two languages concerned, the language teacher will never succeed in teaching his pupils a perfect pronunciation of the new language.

We have seen above that a language is a system of phonemes and prosodemes and that the structure of these systems differs from one language to another. Some systems are richer, others are poorer. Neither the number nor the kind of distinctions used is the same from language to language. The person who begins with a poor vocalic system and must succeed in mastering a richer vocalism, is consequently obliged to learn to make use of acoustic and physiological distinctions which, in his own language, have no functional value. An Englishman or an Italian learning French must learn to use labialization as a distinctive feature. The Spaniard learning English is obliged to learn to make a conscious distinction between a stop [d] and a fricative [ð]. A foreigner who is learning Swedish must get accustomed to making use of musical accent (tone) as an essential feature of the word, and to contrasting a word with accent 1 to a word with accent 2. These are difficulties which in principle are no longer in the area of articulation. It is not labial articulation, nor spirant pronunciation of [ð], nor intonation as such that, in our examples, constitutes difficulties for the foreigner. It is the use of a different phonemic system. It goes without saying that this aspect of learning a foreign pronunciation presupposes an analysis of the two systems in question and a thorough knowledge of the functional structure both of the language to be learned and of that of the pupil.

The problem is in principle the same for the person who speaks a rural dialect or has a strong regional or vulgar accent, and wants to lose it and learn "good" pronunciation. The greater the difference between regional pronunciation and standard pronunciation—from the points of view of articulatory habits and of the functional system—the greater is the difficulty and the more a knowledge of phonetics is necessary.

The invention of different systems of *phonetic transcription*— and especially the creation of the *International Phonetic Alphabet*, used by the *International Phonetic Association* (founded in 1886 by the French phonetician Paul Passy)—has greatly advanced the phonetic teaching of foreign languages. Phonetic transcription allows the pupil to rid himself of spelling and concentrate on phonetic reality. Phonetic writing tends to create as perfect a harmony as possible between the text and the sounds. However, only the vowels and consonants and a limited number of prosodemes figure in a text transcribed phonetically. All the little details of combinatory phonetics, the intonation of the phrase and the rhythmical facts—which are all so important for the general impression that a language gives from the phonetic point of view—are usually completely missing or are at most indicated in an unsatisfactory manner. This fact perhaps explains in part why, in traditional academic phonetics, vowels and consonants have always occupied more place than the prosodic facts (intonation, accents, etc.).

At the present time, new technical inventions like the radio, phonograph and tape recorder are beginning to be used more and more in the teaching of pronunciation. Students can now hear the voices of native speakers pronouncing groups and phrases and can thus immediately form an idea of the auditory image which corresponds to the printed text. Besides, the student can have his own voice recorded and compare his pronunciation with that of the native voice. In this way he discovers his own mistakes much better. It goes without saying that the same method is also employed with great success in the teaching of diction and in the correction of errors of pronunciation in one's native language.

**The language of the deaf and hard of hearing.** The application of phonetics to the teaching of deaf-mutes is also, as may be easily understood, of primary practical interest. A person affected by deafness, either one who is born deaf or who has become deaf before learning to speak,[1] is reduced to using only his muscular sense to learn the articulations necessary for the production of speech sounds. In effect he lacks that constant help of the ear which, in a person with normal hearing, controls and guides his articulation. It is therefore evident that the teacher who is teaching deaf children to speak must know thoroughly all about the physiological aspect of phonetics.

A very large number of deaf people, however, are not deprived of all ability to perceive sound vibrations. They have retained a few traces of hearing which the doctor and the teacher should endeavor to turn to account. It often happens that a partially deaf person hears only certain frequencies to the exclusion of certain others. In cases of this sort, it is necessary to know the acoustics of the sounds of the language in order to know what such a person can perceive in the spectrum of a given sound, and in order to know which frequencies will have to be reinforced so that the sounds of the language may become recognizable to him and so that the distinctions may be sufficiently clear to him to permit a correct identification of phonemes. Phonetics and audiology are at the moment working together in solving the problems posed by the deaf and the hard of hearing.

**Sound transmission.** It is only recently, following discoveries in acoustical phonetics made during these last ten to fifteen years (see above, pp. 87–88), that the technicians of sound

---

[1] Those persons, also, who become deaf at a later age most often need the help of a phonetician in order not to lose their speaking capacity, since they lack the necessary auditory guidance.

transmission have begun to take an interest in phonetics. When someone has to build a machine capable of transmitting the spoken language in one way or another (whether this machine be a microphone, a telephone, a phonograph, or a loud-speaker), he is obliged to know the acoustics of the vowels and consonants if he wants to adjust the mechanism in such a way that it will be able to render all the characteristic vibrations of these sounds. We have seen above that all the frequencies which are met with in speech spectra are not of equal importance to the character of the sound. The formants guarantee its identity and distinguish sounds from each other. The sound engineer will therefore be especially interested in knowing which frequencies are necessary for the identification of phonemes and which are not. He wants to break down the infinitely complex sound wave into a limited number of parameters relevant to the message and to exclude other irrelevant features. The former must necessarily be transmitted by the apparatus; the latter are insignificant and can be omitted. Consequently, a knowledge of the facts of acoustic phonetics can greatly facilitate the work of the engineer.

By an interesting coincidence, the sound engineer is thus trying, on his side, to determine for each sound the same distinctive features which the linguist is looking for, when he tries to establish the functional (structural) system of the language in question. Starting out from entirely different points of view, the technical study of sound and the structural analysis of language have met in a common purpose: the search for the phenomena which convey meaning. At the moment, linguists and technicians are collaborating closely, particularly in the United States, in order to solve together the problems which spoken language poses. Phonetics has thus become an eminently useful science in one more field, an entirely new field and one which up to now has had no connection with linguistics. The traditional boundaries between the different scientific subjects have ceased to exist.

# Bibliography

GENERAL PHONETICS AND GENERAL LINGUISTICS

Bloomfield, L., *Language*. New York, 1950.
Carrell, J. and Tiffany, W. R., *Phonetics: Theory and Application to Speech Improvement*. New York, 1960.
Chiba, T. and Kajiyama, M., *The Vowel, its Nature and Structure*. Tokyo, 1958.
Fant, G., *Acoustic Theory of Speech Production*. Royal Institute of Technology, Report No. 10, Stockholm, 1958.
———, "Modern Instruments and Methods for Acoustic Studies of Speech." *Acta Polytechnica Scandinavica*, Ser. I., Stockholm, 1958.
Fletcher, H., *Speech and Hearing in Communication*. New York, 1953.
Fröschels, E., *Speech Therapy*. Boston, 1933.
Gleason, H. A., Jr., *An Introduction to Descriptive Linguistics*. New York, 1958.
Grammont, M., *Traité de phonétique*. Paris, 1933.
Gray, G. W. and Wise, C. M., *The Bases of Speech*. Rev. ed., New York, 1946.
Harris, Z. S., *Methods in Structural Linguistics*. Chicago, 1951.
Heffner, R.-M. S., *General Phonetics*. Madison, 1960.
Hjelmslev, L., *Prolegomena to a Theory of Language*. 2nd ed., Madison, 1961.
Hocket, C. F., *A Course in Modern Linguistics*. New York, 1958.
Jakobson, R., Fant, G., and Halle, M., *Preliminaries to Speech Analysis*. Massachusetts Institute of Technology, 1952.
Jakobson, R. and Halle, M., *Fundamentals of Language*. 'S-Gravenhage, 1956.
Jones, D., *The Phoneme, Its Nature and Use*. Cambridge, 1950.
Joos, M., "Acoustic Phonetics." Supplement to *Language*, 24:2, 1948.
———, *Readings in Linguistics*. Washington, 1957.
Kantner, C. E. and West, R., *Phonetics*. 5th rev. ed., New York, 1960.
Malmberg, B., *Die Quantität als phonetisch-phonologischer Begriff*. Lund, 1944.
———, *Notas sobre la fonética del español en el Paraguay*. Lund, 1947.
———, *L'espagnol dans le Nouveau Monde—problème de linguistique générale*. Lund, 1948.
———, "Le Problème du classement des sons du langage et quelques questions connexes." In: *Studia Linguistica* VI: 1, Lund, 1952.

Malmberg, B. "The Phonetic Basis for Syllable Division." In: *Studia Linguistica* IX, Lund, 1955.

——, "Observations on the Swedish Word Accent." Haskins Laboratories Report, New York–Lund, 1955.

——, "Questions de méthode en phonétique synchronique." In: *Studia Linguistica* X, Lund, 1956.

Martinet, A., *Phonology as Functional Phonetics*. London, 1949.

——, *Économie des changements phonétiques*. Berne, 1955.

Martinet, A. and Weinreich, U., *Linguistics To-day*. New York, 1954; also in *Word*, X: 2–3, 1954.

Miller, G. A., *Language and Communication*. New York, 1951.

Pike, K. L., *Phonetics*. 3rd pr., Norwood, Mass., 1947.

——, *Tone Languages*. Michigan, 1948.

Potter, R. K., Kopp., G. A., and Green, H. C., *Visible Speech*. New York, 1947.

*The Principles of the International Phonetic Association*. Hertford, 1949 and 1961.

Russel, G. O., *The Vowel*. Columbus, 1928.

Stetson, R. H., *Motor Phonetics. A Study of Speech Movements in Action*. 2nd ed., Amsterdam, 1951.

Twaddell, W. F., "On Defining the Phoneme." *Language Monographs*, publ. by the Linguistic Society of America, Vol. XVI, 1935.

Whatmough, J., *Language*. London, 1956.

Wise, C. M., *Applied Phonetics*. New York, 1957.


ENGLISH PHONETICS

Cohen, A., *The Phonemes of English*. The Hague, 1952.

Colby, F. O., *The American Pronouncing Dictionary of Troublesome Words*. New York, 1950.

Jones, D., *An Outline of English Phonetics*. 7th ed., Cambridge, 1950.

——, *Everyman's English Pronouncing Dictionary*. 11th ed., London, 1956.

Kurath, H. and McDavid, R. I., Jr., *The Pronunciation of English in the Atlantic States*. University of Michigan, 1961.

McCarthy, P., *English Pronunciation*. 4th ed., Cambridge, 1960.

Meyer, E. A., *Englische Lautdauer: eine experimentalphonetische Untersuchung*. Uppsala, 1903.

Pike, K. L., *The Intonation of American English*. Michigan, 1946.

Prator, C. H., Jr., *Manual of American English Pronunciation*. 2nd rev. ed., New York, 1957.

Van Riper, C. G. and Smith, D. E., *An Introduction to General American Phonetics*. New York, 1954.

# Appendix—The International Phonetic Alphabet (Revised to 1951)

## CONSONANTS

| | Bi-labial | Labio-dental | Dental and Alveolar | Retroflex | Palato-alveolar | Alveolo-palatal | Palatal | Velar | Uvular | Pharyngal | Glottal |
|---|---|---|---|---|---|---|---|---|---|---|---|
| Plosive | p b | | t d | ʈ ɖ | | | c ɟ | k g | q ɢ | | ʔ |
| Nasal | m | ɱ | n | ɳ | | | ɲ | ŋ | N | | |
| Lateral Fricative | | | ɬ ɮ | | | | | | | | |
| Lateral Non-fricative | | | l | ɭ | | | ʎ | | | | |
| Rolled | | | r | | | | | | R | | |
| Flapped | | | ɾ | ɽ | | | | | R | | |
| Fricative | ɸ β | f v | θ ð s z ɹ | ʂ ʐ | ʃ ʒ | ɕ ʑ | ç j | x ɣ | χ ʁ | ħ ʕ | h ɦ |
| Frictionless Continuants and Semi-vowels | w ɥ | ʋ | ɹ | | | | j (ɥ) | (w) | ʁ | | |

## VOWELS

| | Bi-labial | | Front | Central | Back |
|---|---|---|---|---|---|
| Close | (y ʉ u) | | i y | ɨ ʉ | ɯ u |
| Half-close | (ø o) | | e ø | ə | ɤ o |
| Half-open | (œ) | | ɛ œ | ɜ æ | ʌ ɔ |
| Open | (ɒ) | | a | ɐ a | ɑ ɒ |

(Secondary articulations are shown by symbols in brackets.)

* This table is reproduced from *The Principles of the International Phonetic Association* (London, 1961), courtesy of the publisher, the International Phonetic Association.

# Index

Absolute quantity, 74
Accent, 80–86; dynamic, 80; expiratory, 80; intensity, 80; musical, 80, 83–86; word, 81
Acoustical instruments, 87, 88
Acoustic classification: of consonants, 15, 16; of the sounds of language, 54, 55; of vowels, 13–15
Acoustic phonetics, 1, 5–20
Acute vowel, 14
Adstratum, 106
Affricated stops, 43
Affricates, 43, 50, 51
Allophones, 93
Altaic languages, 62
Alveolar: articulation, 31; stop, 40
Alveoli, 28
American: English, 34, 36, 45, 47, 104; Indian languages, 35, 41
Amplitude (of vibration), 5 ff., 26, 27
Analogy, 101
Anticipatory assimilation, 61
Apex (of tongue), 28, 31
Aphasia, 108
Apical: articulation, 31; r, 46
Apico-dental stop, 41
Apico-palatal stop, 41
Apophysis: muscular, 23; vocal, 23
Apparatus: respiratory, 21 ff.; speech, 21 ff.
Applications of phonetics, practical, 53, 107–12
Armstrong, 83, 84
Articulation: alveolar, 31; apical, 31; bilabial, 31; dental, 31; dorsal, 31; glottal, 31; labial, 31; labio-dental, 32; laryngeal, 31; medio-palatal, 31; mode of, 41; nasal, 30; oral, 30; pharyngeal, 31; point of, 41; postpalatal, 31; predorsal, 31; prepalatal, 31; types of, 29–32; uvular, 31; velar, 31
Articulatory basis, 71–73, 109
Articulatory classification: of the sounds of language, 53, 54; of vowels, 33–39

Articulatory phonetics, 1
Artificial palate, 89
Arytenoids, 22
Ascoli, Graziadio Isaia, 105
Aspirated voiceless stop, 42
Assimilation, 60–62, 100; anticipatory, 61; contact, 61; distant, 61; double, 61; progressive, 61; regressive, 61
*Atlas linguistique de la France*, 103

Back: of the tongue, 28, 31; r, 46; vowels, 34
Bands, ventricular, 23
Basis, articulatory, 71–73, 109
Beach, 85
Bell, 19
Bilabial: articulation, 31; spirant, 50; stop, 40
Binary oppositions, 54
Bloomfield, Leonard, 93
Boundary, syllabic, 57, 67, 68
Breath groups, 71
British English, 45, 103
Brøndal, 105
Buccal closing, 42

Cavity: labial, 27; mouth, 27; nasal, 27; supraglottal, 27, 28
Center of diffusion, 102
Central vowels, 35
Centring diphthongs, 38
Change, phonetic, 99
Chinese, 85
Chroneme, 96
Classification of consonants, acoustic, 15, 16
Classification of the sounds of language, 53–55; acoustic, 54, 55; articulatory, 53, 54
Classification of vowels: acoustic, 13–15; articulatory, 33–39
Click, 29; glottalic, 29
Closed syllable, 65
Close vowel, 34 and *passim*
Closing: buccal, 42; diphthongs, 38

117

# A CATALOGUE OF SELECTED DOVER BOOKS
## IN ALL FIELDS OF INTEREST

# A CATALOGUE OF SELECTED DOVER BOOKS
## IN ALL FIELDS OF INTEREST

LEATHER TOOLING AND CARVING, Chris H. Groneman. One of few books concentrating on tooling and carving, with complete instructions and grid designs for 39 projects ranging from bookmarks to bags. 148 illustrations. 111pp. 7⅞ x 10.
23061-9 Pa. $2.50

THE CODEX NUTTALL, A PICTURE MANUSCRIPT FROM ANCIENT MEXICO, as first edited by Zelia Nuttall. Only inexpensive edition, in full color, of a pre-Columbian Mexican (Mixtec) book. 88 color plates show kings, gods, heroes, temples, sacrifices. New explanatory, historical introduction by Arthur G. Miller. 96pp. 11⅜ x 8½.
23168-2 Pa. $7.50

AMERICAN PRIMITIVE PAINTING, Jean Lipman. Classic collection of an enduring American tradition. 109 plates, 8 in full color—portraits, landscapes, Biblical and historical scenes, etc., showing family groups, farm life, and so on. 80pp. of lucid text. 8⅜ x 11¼.
22815-0 Pa. $5.00

WILL BRADLEY: HIS GRAPHIC ART, edited by Clarence P. Hornung. Striking collection of work by foremost practitioner of Art Nouveau in America: posters, cover designs, sample pages, advertisements, other illustrations. 97 plates, including 8 in full color and 19 in two colors. 97pp. 9⅜ x 12¼.
20701-3 Pa. $4.00
22120-2 Clothbd. $10.00

AN ATLAS OF ANATOMY FOR ARTISTS, Fritz Schider. Finest text, working book. Full text, plus anatomical illustrations; plates by great artists showing anatomy. 593 illustrations. 192pp. 7⅞ x 10¾.
20241-0 Clothbd. $6.95

THE GIBSON GIRL AND HER AMERICA, Charles Dana Gibson. 155 finest drawings of effervescent world of 1900-1910: the Gibson Girl and her loves, amusements, adventures, Mr. Pipp, etc. Selected by E. Gillon; introduction by Henry Pitz. 144pp. 8¼ x 11⅜.
21986-0 Pa. $3.50

STAINED GLASS CRAFT, J.A.F. Divine, G. Blachford. One of the very few books that tell the beginner exactly what he needs to know: planning cuts, making shapes, avoiding design weaknesses, fitting glass, etc. 93 illustrations. 115pp.
22812-6 Pa. $1.75

CREATIVE LITHOGRAPHY AND HOW TO DO IT, Grant Arnold. Lithography as art form: working directly on stone, transfer of drawings, lithotint, mezzotint, color printing; also metal plates. Detailed, thorough. 27 illustrations. 214pp.
21208-4 Pa. $3.50

DESIGN MOTIFS OF ANCIENT MEXICO, Jorge Enciso. Vigorous, powerful ceramic stamp impressions — Maya, Aztec, Toltec, Olmec. Serpents, gods, priests, dancers, etc. 153pp. 6⅛ x 9¼. 20084-1 Pa. $2.50

AMERICAN INDIAN DESIGN AND DECORATION, Leroy Appleton. Full text, plus more than 700 precise drawings of Inca, Maya, Aztec, Pueblo, Plains, NW Coast basketry, sculpture, painting, pottery, sand paintings, metal, etc. 4 plates in color. 279pp. 8⅜ x 11¼. 22704-9 Pa.$5.00

CHINESE LATTICE DESIGNS, Daniel S. Dye. Incredibly beautiful geometric designs: circles, voluted, simple dissections, etc. Inexhaustible source of ideas, motifs. 1239 illustrations. 469pp. 6⅛ x 9¼. 23096-1 Pa. $5.00

JAPANESE DESIGN MOTIFS, Matsuya Co. Mon, or heraldic designs. Over 4000 typical, beautiful designs: birds, animals, flowers, swords, fans, geometric; all beautifully stylized. 213pp. 11⅜ x 8¼. 22874-6 Pa. $5.00

PERSPECTIVE, Jan Vredeman de Vries. 73 perspective plates from 1604 edition; buildings, townscapes, stairways, fantastic scenes. Remarkable for beauty, surrealistic atmosphere; real eye-catchers. Introduction by Adolf Placzek. 74pp. 11⅜ x 8¼. 20186-4 Pa. $2.75

EARLY AMERICAN DESIGN MOTIFS. Suzanne E. Chapman. 497 motifs, designs, from painting on wood, ceramics, appliqué, glassware, samplers, metal work, etc. Florals, landscapes, birds and animals, geometrics, letters, etc. Inexhaustible. Enlarged edition. 138pp. 8⅜ x 11¼. 22985-8 Pa. $3.50
23084-8 Clothbd. $7.95

VICTORIAN STENCILS FOR DESIGN AND DECORATION, edited by E.V. Gillon, Jr. 113 wonderful ornate Victorian pieces from German sources; florals, geometrics; borders, corner pieces; bird motifs, etc. 64pp. 9⅜ x 12¼. 21995-X Pa. $3.00

ART NOUVEAU: AN ANTHOLOGY OF DESIGN AND ILLUSTRATION FROM THE STUDIO, edited by E.V. Gillon, Jr. Graphic arts: book jackets, posters, engravings, illustrations, decorations; Crane, Beardsley, Bradley and many others. Inexhaustible. 92pp. 8⅛ x 11. 22388-4 Pa. $2.50

ORIGINAL ART DECO DESIGNS, William Rowe. First-rate, highly imaginative modern Art Deco frames, borders, compositions, alphabets, florals, insectals, Wurlitzer-types, etc. Much finest modern Art Deco. 80 plates, 8 in color. 8⅜ x 11¼. 22567-4 Pa. $3.50

HANDBOOK OF DESIGNS AND DEVICES, Clarence P. Hornung. Over 1800 basic geometric designs based on circle, triangle, square, scroll, cross, etc. Largest such collection in existence. 261pp. 20125-2 Pa. $2.75

150 MASTERPIECES OF DRAWING, edited by Anthony Toney. 150 plates, early 15th century to end of 18th century; Rembrandt, Michelangelo, Dürer, Fragonard, Watteau, Wouwerman, many others. 150pp. 8⅜ x 11¼.　　21032-4 Pa. $4.00

THE GOLDEN AGE OF THE POSTER, Hayward and Blanche Cirker. 70 extraordinary posters in full colors, from Maîtres de l'Affiche, Mucha, Lautrec, Bradley, Cheret, Beardsley, many others. 9⅜ x 12¼.　　22753-7 Pa. $5.95
21718-3 Clothbd. $7.95

SIMPLICISSIMUS, selection, translations and text by Stanley Appelbaum. 180 satirical drawings, 16 in full color, from the famous German weekly magazine in the years 1896 to 1926. 24 artists included: Grosz, Kley, Pascin, Kubin, Kollwitz, plus Heine, Thöny, Bruno Paul, others. 172pp. 8½ x 12¼.　　23098-8 Pa. $5.00
23099-6 Clothbd. $10.00

THE EARLY WORK OF AUBREY BEARDSLEY, Aubrey Beardsley. 157 plates, 2 in color: Manon Lescaut, Madame Bovary, Morte d'Arthur, Salome, other. Introduction by H. Marillier. 175pp. 8½ x 11.　　21816-3 Pa. $4.00

THE LATER WORK OF AUBREY BEARDSLEY, Aubrey Beardsley. Exotic masterpieces of full maturity: Venus and Tannhäuser, Lysistrata, Rape of the Lock, Volpone, Savoy material, etc. 174 plates, 2 in color. 176pp. 8½ x 11. 21817-1 Pa. $4.00

DRAWINGS OF WILLIAM BLAKE, William Blake. 92 plates from Book of Job, Divine Comedy, Paradise Lost, visionary heads, mythological figures, Laocoön, etc. Selection, introduction, commentary by Sir Geoffrey Keynes. 178pp. 8½ x 11.
22303-5 Pa. $4.00

LONDON: A PILGRIMAGE, Gustave Doré, Blanchard Jerrold. Squalor, riches, misery, beauty of mid-Victorian metropolis; 55 wonderful plates, 125 other illustrations, full social, cultural text by Jerrold. 191pp. of text. 8⅛ x 11.
22306-X Pa. $6.00

THE COMPLETE WOODCUTS OF ALBRECHT DÜRER, edited by Dr. W. Kurth. 346 in all: Old Testament, St. Jerome, Passion, Life of Virgin, Apocalypse, many others. Introduction by Campbell Dodgson. 285pp. 8½ x 12¼.　　21097-9 Pa. $6.00

THE DISASTERS OF WAR, Francisco Goya. 83 etchings record horrors of Napoleonic wars in Spain and war in general. Reprint of 1st edition, plus 3 additional plates. Introduction by Philip Hofer. 97pp. 9⅜ x 8¼.　　21872-4 Pa. $3.50

ENGRAVINGS OF HOGARTH, William Hogarth. 101 of Hogarth's greatest works: Rake's Progress, Harlot's Progress, Illustrations for Hudibras, Midnight Modern Conversation, Before and After, Beer Street and Gin Lane, many more. Full commentary. 256pp. 11 x 14.　　22479-1 Pa. $7.95,

PRIMITIVE ART, Franz Boas. Great anthropologist on ceramics, textiles, wood, stone, metal, etc.; patterns, technology, symbols, styles. All areas, but fullest on Northwest Coast Indians. 350 illustrations. 378pp.　　20025-6 Pa. $3.75

MOTHER GOOSE'S MELODIES. Facsimile of fabulously rare Munroe and Francis "copyright 1833" Boston edition. Familiar and unusual rhymes, wonderful old woodcut illustrations. Edited by E.F. Bleiler. 128pp. 4½ x 6⅜. 22577-1 Pa. $1.50

MOTHER GOOSE IN HIEROGLYPHICS. Favorite nursery rhymes presented in rebus form for children. Fascinating 1849 edition reproduced in toto, with key. Introduction by E.F. Bleiler. About 400 woodcuts. 64pp. 6⅞ x 5¼. 20745-5 Pa. $1.50

PETER PIPER'S PRACTICAL PRINCIPLES OF PLAIN & PERFECT PRONUNCIATION. Alliterative jingles and tongue-twisters. Reproduction in full of 1830 first American edition. 25 spirited woodcuts. 32pp. 4½ x 6⅜. 22560-7 Pa. $1.25

THE NIGHT BEFORE CHRISTMAS, Clement Moore. Full text, and woodcuts from original 1848 book. Also critical, historical material. 19 illustrations. 40pp. 4⅝ x 6. 22797-9 Pa. $1.35

THE KING OF THE GOLDEN RIVER, John Ruskin. Victorian children's classic of three brothers, their attempts to reach the Golden River, what becomes of them. Facsimile of original 1889 edition. 22 illustrations. 56pp. 4⅝ x 6⅜. 20066-3 Pa. $1.50

DREAMS OF THE RAREBIT FIEND, Winsor McCay. Pioneer cartoon strip, unexcelled for beauty, imagination, in 60 full sequences. Incredible technical virtuosity, wonderful visual wit. Historical introduction. 62pp. 8⅜ x 11¼. 21347-1 Pa. $2.50

THE KATZENJAMMER KIDS, Rudolf Dirks. In full color, 14 strips from 1906-7; full of imagination, characteristic humor. Classic of great historical importance. Introduction by August Derleth. 32pp. 9¼ x 12¼. 23005-8 Pa. $2.00

LITTLE ORPHAN ANNIE AND LITTLE ORPHAN ANNIE IN COSMIC CITY, Harold Gray. Two great sequences from the early strips: our curly-haired heroine defends the Warbucks' financial empire and, then, takes on meanie Phineas P. Pinchpenny. Leapin' lizards! 178pp. 6⅛ x 8⅜. 23107-0 Pa. $2.00

WHEN A FELLER NEEDS A FRIEND, Clare Briggs. 122 cartoons by one of the greatest newspaper cartoonists of the early 20th century — about growing up, making a living, family life, daily frustrations and occasional triumphs. 121pp. 8½ x 9½. 23148-8 Pa. $2.50

ABSOLUTELY MAD INVENTIONS, A.E. Brown, H.A. Jeffcott. Hilarious, useless, or merely absurd inventions all granted patents by the U.S. Patent Office. Edible tie pin, mechanical hat tipper, etc. 57 illustrations. 125pp. 22596-8 Pa. $1.50

THE DEVIL'S DICTIONARY, Ambrose Bierce. Barbed, bitter, brilliant witticisms in the form of a dictionary. Best, most ferocious satire America has produced. 145pp. 20487-1 Pa. $1.75

THE BEST DR. THORNDYKE DETECTIVE STORIES, R. Austin Freeman. The Case of Oscar Brodski, The Moabite Cipher, and 5 other favorites featuring the great scientific detective, plus his long-believed-lost first adventure — 31 New Inn — reprinted here for the first time. Edited by E.F. Bleiler. USO 20388-3 Pa. $3.00

BEST "THINKING MACHINE" DETECTIVE STORIES, Jacques Futrelle. The Problem of Cell 13 and 11 other stories about Prof. Augustus S.F.X. Van Dusen, including two "lost" stories. First reprinting of several. Edited by E.F. Bleiler. 241pp.
20537-1 Pa. $3.00

UNCLE SILAS, J. Sheridan LeFanu. Victorian Gothic mystery novel, considered by many best of period, even better than Collins or Dickens. Wonderful psychological terror. Introduction by Frederick Shroyer. 436pp. 21715-9 Pa. $4.00

BEST DR. POGGIOLI DETECTIVE STORIES, T.S. Stribling. 15 best stories from EQMM and The Saint offer new adventures in Mexico, Florida, Tennessee hills as Poggioli unravels mysteries and combats Count Jalacki. 217pp. 23227-1 Pa. $3.00

EIGHT DIME NOVELS, selected with an introduction by E.F. Bleiler. Adventures of Old King Brady, Frank James, Nick Carter, Deadwood Dick, Buffalo Bill, The Steam Man, Frank Merriwell, and Horatio Alger — 1877 to 1905. Important, entertaining popular literature in facsimile reprint, with original covers. 190pp. 9 x 12.
22975-0 Pa. $3.50

ALICE'S ADVENTURES UNDER GROUND, Lewis Carroll. Facsimile of ms. Carroll gave Alice Liddell in 1864. Different in many ways from final Alice. Handlettered, illustrated by Carroll. Introduction by Martin Gardner. 128pp. 21482-6 Pa. $2.00

ALICE IN WONDERLAND COLORING BOOK, Lewis Carroll. Pictures by John Tenniel. Large-size versions of the famous illustrations of Alice, Cheshire Cat, Mad Hatter and all the others, waiting for your crayons. Abridged text. 36 illustrations. 64pp. 8¼ x 11.
22853-3 Pa. $1.50

AVENTURES D'ALICE AU PAYS DES MERVEILLES, Lewis Carroll. Bué's translation of "Alice" into French, supervised by Carroll himself. Novel way to learn language. (No English text.) 42 Tenniel illustrations. 196pp. 22836-3 Pa. $3.00

MYTHS AND FOLK TALES OF IRELAND, Jeremiah Curtin. 11 stories that are Irish versions of European fairy tales and 9 stories from the Fenian cycle — 20 tales of legend and magic that comprise an essential work in the history of folklore. 256pp.
22430-9 Pa. $3.00

EAST O' THE SUN AND WEST O' THE MOON, George W. Dasent. Only full edition of favorite, wonderful Norwegian fairytales — Why the Sea is Salt, Boots and the Troll, etc. — with 77 illustrations by Kittelsen & Werenskiöld. 418pp.
22521-6 Pa. $4.50

PERRAULT'S FAIRY TALES, Charles Perrault and Gustave Doré. Original versions of Cinderella, Sleeping Beauty, Little Red Riding Hood, etc. in best translation, with 34 wonderful illustrations by Gustave Doré. 117pp. 8⅛ x 11. 22311-6 Pa. $2.50

EARLY NEW ENGLAND GRAVESTONE RUBBINGS, Edmund V. Gillon, Jr. 43 photographs, 226 rubbings show heavily symbolic, macabre, sometimes humorous primitive American art. Up to early 19th century. 207pp. 8⅜ x 11¼.
21380-3 Pa. $4.00

L.J.M. DAGUERRE: THE HISTORY OF THE DIORAMA AND THE DAGUERREOTYPE, Helmut and Alison Gernsheim. Definitive account. Early history, life and work of Daguerre; discovery of daguerreotype process; diffusion abroad; other early photography. 124 illustrations. 226pp. 6⅙ x 9¼.
22290-X Pa. $4.00

PHOTOGRAPHY AND THE AMERICAN SCENE, Robert Taft. The basic book on American photography as art, recording form, 1839-1889. Development, influence on society, great photographers, types (portraits, war, frontier, etc.), whatever else needed. Inexhaustible. Illustrated with 322 early photos, daguerreotypes, tintypes, stereo slides, etc. 546pp. 6⅛ x 9¼.
21201-7 Pa. $5.95

PHOTOGRAPHIC SKETCHBOOK OF THE CIVIL WAR, Alexander Gardner. Reproduction of 1866 volume with 100 on-the-field photographs: Manassas, Lincoln on battlefield, slave pens, etc. Introduction by E.F. Bleiler. 224pp. 10¾ x 9.
22731-6 Pa. $6.00

THE MOVIES: A PICTURE QUIZ BOOK, Stanley Appelbaum & Hayward Cirker. Match stars with their movies, name actors and actresses, test your movie skill with 241 stills from 236 great movies, 1902-1959. Indexes of performers and films. 128pp. 8⅜ x 9¼.
20222-4 Pa. $2.50

THE TALKIES, Richard Griffith. Anthology of features, articles from Photoplay, 1928-1940, reproduced complete. Stars, famous movies, technical features, fabulous ads, etc.; Garbo, Chaplin, King Kong, Lubitsch, etc. 4 color plates, scores of illustrations. 327pp. 8⅜ x 11¼.
22762-6 Pa. $6.95

THE MOVIE MUSICAL FROM VITAPHONE TO "42ND STREET," edited by Miles Kreuger. Relive the rise of the movie musical as reported in the pages of Photoplay magazine (1926-1933): every movie review, cast list, ad, and record review; every significant feature article, production still, biography, forecast, and gossip story. Profusely illustrated. 367pp. 8⅜ x 11¼.
23154-2 Pa. $7.95

JOHANN SEBASTIAN BACH, Philipp Spitta. Great classic of biography, musical commentary, with hundreds of pieces analyzed. Also good for Bach's contemporaries. 450 musical examples. Total of 1799pp.
EUK 22278-0, 22279-9 Clothbd., Two vol. set $25.00

BEETHOVEN AND HIS NINE SYMPHONIES, Sir George Grove. Thorough history, analysis, commentary on symphonies and some related pieces. For either beginner or advanced student. 436 musical passages. 407pp.
20334-4 Pa. $4.00

MOZART AND HIS PIANO CONCERTOS, Cuthbert Girdlestone. The only full-length study. Detailed analyses of all 21 concertos, sources; 417 musical examples. 509pp.
21271-8 Pa. $6.00

THE FITZWILLIAM VIRGINAL BOOK, edited by J. Fuller Maitland, W.B. Squire. Famous early 17th century collection of keyboard music, 300 works by Morley, Byrd, Bull, Gibbons, etc. Modern notation. Total of 938pp. 8⅜ x 11.
ECE 21068-5, 21069-3 Pa., Two vol. set $15.00

COMPLETE STRING QUARTETS, Wolfgang A. Mozart. Breitkopf and Härtel edition. All 23 string quartets plus alternate slow movement to K156. Study score. 277pp. 9⅜ x 12¼.
22372-8 Pa. $6.00

COMPLETE SONG CYCLES, Franz Schubert. Complete piano, vocal music of Die Schöne Müllerin, Die Winterreise, Schwanengesang. Also Drinker English singing translations. Breitkopf and Härtel edition. 217pp. 9⅜ x 12¼.
22649-2 Pa. $5.00

THE COMPLETE PRELUDES AND ETUDES FOR PIANOFORTE SOLO, Alexander Scriabin. All the preludes and etudes including many perfectly spun miniatures. Edited by K.N. Igumnov and Y.I. Mil'shteyn. 250pp. 9 x 12.
22919-X Pa. $6.00

TRISTAN UND ISOLDE, Richard Wagner. Full orchestral score with complete instrumentation. Do not confuse with piano reduction. Commentary by Felix Mottl, great Wagnerian conductor and scholar. Study score. 655pp. 8⅛ x 11.
22915-7 Pa. $11.95

FAVORITE SONGS OF THE NINETIES, ed. Robert Fremont. Full reproduction, including covers, of 88 favorites: Ta-Ra-Ra-Boom-De-Aye, The Band Played On, Bird in a Gilded Cage, Under the Bamboo Tree, After the Ball, etc. 401pp. 9 x 12.
EBE 21536-9 Pa. $6.95

SOUSA'S GREAT MARCHES IN PIANO TRANSCRIPTION: ORIGINAL SHEET MUSIC OF 23 WORKS, John Philip Sousa. Selected by Lester S. Levy. Playing edition includes: The Stars and Stripes Forever, The Thunderer, The Gladiator, King Cotton, Washington Post, much more. 24 illustrations. 111pp. 9 x 12.
USO 23132-1 Pa. $3.50

CLASSIC PIANO RAGS, selected with an introduction by Rudi Blesh. Best ragtime music (1897-1922) by Scott Joplin, James Scott, Joseph F. Lamb, Tom Turpin, 9 others. Printed from best original sheet music, plus covers. 364pp. 9 x 12.
EBE 20469-3 Pa. $7.50

ANALYSIS OF CHINESE CHARACTERS, C.D. Wilder, J.H. Ingram. 1000 most important characters analyzed according to primitives, phonetics, historical development. Traditional method offers mnemonic aid to beginner, intermediate student of Chinese, Japanese. 365pp.
23045-7 Pa. $4.00

MODERN CHINESE: A BASIC COURSE, Faculty of Peking University. Self study, classroom course in modern Mandarin. Records contain phonetics, vocabulary, sentences, lessons. 249 page book contains all recorded text, translations, grammar, vocabulary, exercises. Best course on market. 3 12" 33⅓ monaural records, book, album.
98832-5 Set $12.50

MANUAL OF THE TREES OF NORTH AMERICA, Charles S. Sargent. The basic survey of every native tree and tree-like shrub, 717 species in all. Extremely full descriptions, information on habitat, growth, locales, economics, etc. Necessary to every serious tree lover. Over 100 finding keys. 783 illustrations. Total of 986pp.
20277-1, 20278-X Pa., Two vol. set $9.00

BIRDS OF THE NEW YORK AREA, John Bull. Indispensable guide to more than 400 species within a hundred-mile radius of Manhattan. Information on range, status, breeding, migration, distribution trends, etc. Foreword by Roger Tory Peterson. 17 drawings; maps. 540pp. 23222-0 Pa. $6.00

THE SEA-BEACH AT EBB-TIDE, Augusta Foote Arnold. Identify hundreds of marine plants and animals: algae, seaweeds, squids, crabs, corals, etc. Descriptions cover food, life cycle, size, shape, habitat. Over 600 drawings. 490pp.
21949-6 Pa. $5.00

THE MOTH BOOK, William J. Holland. Identify more than 2,000 moths of North America. General information, precise species descriptions. 623 illustrations plus 48 color plates show almost all species, full size. 1968 edition. Still the basic book. Total of 551pp. 6½ x 9¼. 21948-8 Pa. $6.00

HOW INDIANS USE WILD PLANTS FOR FOOD, MEDICINE & CRAFTS, Frances Densmore. Smithsonian, Bureau of American Ethnology report presents wealth of material on nearly 200 plants used by Chippewas of Minnesota and Wisconsin. 33 plates plus 122pp. of text. 6⅛ x 9¼. 23019-8 Pa. $2.50

OLD NEW YORK IN EARLY PHOTOGRAPHS, edited by Mary Black. Your only chance to see New York City as it was 1853-1906, through 196 wonderful photographs from N.Y. Historical Society. Great Blizzard, Lincoln's funeral procession, great buildings. 228pp. 9 x 12. 22907-6 Pa. $6.95

THE AMERICAN REVOLUTION, A PICTURE SOURCEBOOK, John Grafton. Wonderful Bicentennial picture source, with 411 illustrations (contemporary and 19th century) showing battles, personalities, maps, events, flags, posters, soldier's life, ships, etc. all captioned and explained. A wonderful browsing book, supplement to other historical reading. 160pp. 9 x 12. 23226-3 Pa. $4.00

PERSONAL NARRATIVE OF A PILGRIMAGE TO AL-MADINAH AND MECCAH, Richard Burton. Great travel classic by remarkably colorful personality. Burton, disguised as a Moroccan, visited sacred shrines of Islam, narrowly escaping death. Wonderful observations of Islamic life, customs, personalities. 47 illustrations. Total of 959pp. 21217-3, 21218-1 Pa., Two vol. set $10.00

INCIDENTS OF TRAVEL IN CENTRAL AMERICA, CHIAPAS, AND YUCATAN, John L. Stephens. Almost single-handed discovery of Maya culture; exploration of ruined cities, monuments, temples; customs of Indians. 115 drawings. 892pp.
22404-X, 22405-8 Pa., Two vol. set $9.00

CONSTRUCTION OF AMERICAN FURNITURE TREASURES, Lester Margon. 344 detail drawings, complete text on constructing exact reproductions of 38 early American masterpieces: Hepplewhite sideboard, Duncan Phyfe drop-leaf table, mantel clock, gate-leg dining table, Pa. German cupboard, more. 38 plates. 54 photographs. 168pp. 8⅜ x 11¼. 23056-2 Pa. $4.00

JEWELRY MAKING AND DESIGN, Augustus F. Rose, Antonio Cirino. Professional secrets revealed in thorough, practical guide: tools, materials, processes; rings, brooches, chains, cast pieces, enamelling, setting stones, etc. Do not confuse with skimpy introductions: beginner can use, professional can learn from it. Over 200 illustrations. 306pp. 21750-7 Pa. $3.00

METALWORK AND ENAMELLING, Herbert Maryon. Generally conceded best all-around book. Countless trade secrets: materials, tools, soldering, filigree, setting, inlay, niello, repoussé, casting, polishing, etc. For beginner or expert. Author was foremost British expert. 330 illustrations. 335pp. 22702-2 Pa. $4.00

WEAVING WITH FOOT-POWER LOOMS, Edward F. Worst. Setting up a loom, beginning to weave, constructing equipment, using dyes, more, plus over 285 drafts of traditional patterns including Colonial and Swedish weaves. More than 200 other figures. For beginning and advanced. 275pp. 8¾ x 6⅜. 23064-3 Pa. $4.50

WEAVING A NAVAJO BLANKET, Gladys A. Reichard. Foremost anthropologist studied under Navajo women, reveals every step in process from wool, dyeing, spinning, setting up loom, designing, weaving. Much history, symbolism. With this book you could make one yourself. 97 illustrations. 222pp. 22992-0 Pa. $3.00

NATURAL DYES AND HOME DYEING, Rita J. Adrosko. Use natural ingredients: bark, flowers, leaves, lichens, insects etc. Over 135 specific recipes from historical sources for cotton, wool, other fabrics. Genuine premodern handicrafts. 12 illustrations. 160pp. 22688-3 Pa. $2.00

DRIED FLOWERS, Sarah Whitlock and Martha Rankin. Concise, clear, practical guide to dehydration, glycerinizing, pressing plant material, and more. Covers use of silica gel. 12 drawings. Originally titled "New Techniques with Dried Flowers." 32pp. 21802-3 Pa. $1.00

THOMAS NAST: CARTOONS AND ILLUSTRATIONS, with text by Thomas Nast St. Hill. Father of American political cartooning. Cartoons that destroyed Tweed Ring; inflation, free love, church and state; original Republican elephant and Democratic donkey; Santa Claus; more. 117 illustrations. 146pp. 9 x 12.
22983-1 Pa. $4.00
23067-8 Clothbd. $8.50

FREDERIC REMINGTON: 173 DRAWINGS AND ILLUSTRATIONS. Most famous of the Western artists, most responsible for our myths about the American West in its untamed days. Complete reprinting of *Drawings of Frederic Remington* (1897), plus other selections. 4 additional drawings in color on covers. 140pp. 9 x 12.
20714-5 Pa. $5.00

How to Solve Chess Problems, Kenneth S. Howard. Practical suggestions on problem solving for very beginners. 58 two-move problems, 46 3-movers, 8 4-movers for practice, plus hints. 171pp.  20748-X Pa. $3.00

A Guide to Fairy Chess, Anthony Dickins. 3-D chess, 4-D chess, chess on a cylindrical board, reflecting pieces that bounce off edges, cooperative chess, retrograde chess, maximummers, much more. Most based on work of great Dawson. Full handbook, 100 problems. 66pp. 7⅞ x 10¾.  22687-5 Pa. $2.00

Win at Backgammon, Millard Hopper. Best opening moves, running game, blocking game, back game, tables of odds, etc. Hopper makes the game clear enough for anyone to play, and win. 43 diagrams. 111pp.  22894-0 Pa. $1.50

Bidding a Bridge Hand, Terence Reese. Master player "thinks out loud" the binding of 75 hands that defy point count systems. Organized by bidding problem—no-fit situations, overbidding, underbidding, cueing your defense, etc. 254pp.  EBE 22830-4 Pa. $3.00

The Precision Bidding System in Bridge, C.C. Wei, edited by Alan Truscott. Inventor of precision bidding presents average hands and hands from actual play, including games from 1969 Bermuda Bowl where system emerged. 114 exercises. 116pp.  21171-1 Pa. $1.75

Learn Magic, Henry Hay. 20 simple, easy-to-follow lessons on magic for the new magician: illusions, card tricks, silks, sleights of hand, coin manipulations, escapes, and more —all with a minimum amount of equipment. Final chapter explains the great stage illusions. 92 illustrations. 285pp.  21238-6 Pa. $2.95

The New Magician's Manual, Walter B. Gibson. Step-by-step instructions and clear illustrations guide the novice in mastering 36 tricks; much equipment supplied on 16 pages of cut-out materials. 36 additional tricks. 64 illustrations. 159pp. 6⅝ x 10.  23113-5 Pa. $3.00

Professional Magic for Amateurs, Walter B. Gibson. 50 easy, effective tricks used by professionals —cards, string, tumblers, handkerchiefs, mental magic, etc. 63 illustrations. 223pp.  23012-0 Pa. $2.50

Card Manipulations, Jean Hugard. Very rich collection of manipulations; has taught thousands of fine magicians tricks that are really workable, eye-catching. Easily followed, serious work. Over 200 illustrations. 163pp. 20539-8 Pa. $2.00

Abbott's Encyclopedia of Rope Tricks for Magicians, Stewart James. Complete reference book for amateur and professional magicians containing more than 150 tricks involving knots, penetrations, cut and restored rope, etc. 510 illustrations. Reprint of 3rd edition. 400pp.  23206-9 Pa. $3.50

The Secrets of Houdini, J.C. Cannell. Classic study of Houdini's incredible magic, exposing closely-kept professional secrets and revealing, in general terms, the whole art of stage magic. 67 illustrations. 279pp.  22913-0 Pa. $3.00

THE MAGIC MOVING PICTURE BOOK, Bliss, Sands & Co. The pictures in this book move! Volcanoes erupt, a house burns, a serpentine dancer wiggles her way through a number. By using a specially ruled acetate screen provided, you can obtain these and 15 other startling effects. Originally "The Motograph Moving Picture Book." 32pp. 8¼ x 11. 23224-7 Pa. $1.75

STRING FIGURES AND HOW TO MAKE THEM, Caroline F. Jayne. Fullest, clearest instructions on string figures from around world: Eskimo, Navajo, Lapp, Europe, more. Cats cradle, moving spear, lightning, stars. Introduction by A.C. Haddon. 950 illustrations. 407pp. 20152-X Pa. $3.50

PAPER FOLDING FOR BEGINNERS, William D. Murray and Francis J. Rigney. Clearest book on market for making origami sail boats, roosters, frogs that move legs, cups, bonbon boxes. 40 projects. More than 275 illustrations. Photographs. 94pp. 20713-7 Pa. $1.25

INDIAN SIGN LANGUAGE, William Tomkins. Over 525 signs developed by Sioux, Blackfoot, Cheyenne, Arapahoe and other tribes. Written instructions and diagrams: how to make words, construct sentences. Also 290 pictographs of Sioux and Ojibway tribes. 111pp. 6⅛ x 9¼. 22029-X Pa. $1.75

BOOMERANGS: HOW TO MAKE AND THROW THEM, Bernard S. Mason. Easy to make and throw, dozens of designs: cross-stick, pinwheel, boomabird, tumblestick, Australian curved stick boomerang. Complete throwing instructions. All safe. 99pp. 23028-7 Pa. $1.75

25 KITES THAT FLY, Leslie Hunt. Full, easy to follow instructions for kites made from inexpensive materials. Many novelties. Reeling, raising, designing your own. 70 illustrations. 110pp. 22550-X Pa. $1.50

TRICKS AND GAMES ON THE POOL TABLE, Fred Herrmann. 79 tricks and games, some solitaires, some for 2 or more players, some competitive; mystifying shots and throws, unusual carom, tricks involving cork, coins, a hat, more. 77 figures. 95pp. 21814-7 Pa. $1.50

WOODCRAFT AND CAMPING, Bernard S. Mason. How to make a quick emergency shelter, select woods that will burn immediately, make do with limited supplies, etc. Also making many things out of wood, rawhide, bark, at camp. Formerly titled Woodcraft. 295 illustrations. 580pp. 21951-8 Pa. $4.00

AN INTRODUCTION TO CHESS MOVES AND TACTICS SIMPLY EXPLAINED, Leonard Barden. Informal intermediate introduction: reasons for moves, tactics, openings, traps, positional play, endgame. Isolates patterns. 102pp. USO 21210-6 Pa. $1.35

LASKER'S MANUAL OF CHESS, Dr. Emanuel Lasker. Great world champion offers very thorough coverage of all aspects of chess. Combinations, position play, openings, endgame, aesthetics of chess, philosophy of struggle, much more. Filled with analyzed games. 390pp. 20640-8 Pa. $4.00

SLEEPING BEAUTY, illustrated by Arthur Rackham. Perhaps the fullest, most delightful version ever, told by C.S. Evans. Rackham's best work. 49 illustrations. 110pp. 7⅞ x 10¾.                                                      22756-1 Pa. $2.00

THE WONDERFUL WIZARD OF OZ, L. Frank Baum. Facsimile in full color of America's finest children's classic. Introduction by Martin Gardner. 143 illustrations by W.W. Denslow. 267pp.                                              20691-2 Pa. $3.00

GOOPS AND HOW TO BE THEM, Gelett Burgess. Classic tongue-in-cheek masquerading as etiquette book. 87 verses, 170 cartoons as Goops demonstrate virtues of table manners, neatness, courtesy, more. 88pp. 6½ x 9¼.
22233-0 Pa. $2.00

THE BROWNIES, THEIR BOOK, Palmer Cox. Small as mice, cunning as foxes, exuberant, mischievous, Brownies go to zoo, toy shop, seashore, circus, more. 24 verse adventures. 266 illustrations. 144pp. 6⅝ x 9¼.      21265-3 Pa. $2.50

BILLY WHISKERS: THE AUTOBIOGRAPHY OF A GOAT, Frances Trego Montgomery. Escapades of that rambunctious goat. Favorite from turn of the century America. 24 illustrations. 259pp.                                              22345-0 Pa. $2.75

THE ROCKET BOOK, Peter Newell. Fritz, janitor's kid, sets off rocket in basement of apartment house; an ingenious hole punched through every page traces course of rocket. 22 duotone drawings, verses. 48pp. 6⅞ x 8⅜.       22044-3 Pa. $1.50

CUT AND COLOR PAPER MASKS, Michael Grater. Clowns, animals, funny faces . . . simply color them in, cut them out, and put them together, and you have 9 paper masks to play with and enjoy. Complete instructions. Assembled masks shown in full color on the covers. 32pp. 8¼ x 11.      23171-2 Pa. $1.50

THE TALE OF PETER RABBIT, Beatrix Potter. The inimitable Peter's terrifying adventure in Mr. McGregor's garden, with all 27 wonderful, full-color Potter illustrations. 55pp. 4¼ x 5½.                              USO 22827-4 Pa. $1.00

THE TALE OF MRS. TIGGY-WINKLE, Beatrix Potter. Your child will love this story about a very special hedgehog and all 27 wonderful, full-color Potter illustrations. 57pp. 4¼ x 5½.                              USO 20546-0 Pa. $1.00

THE TALE OF BENJAMIN BUNNY, Beatrix Potter. Peter Rabbit's cousin coaxes him back into Mr. McGregor's garden for a whole new set of adventures. A favorite with children. All 27 full-color illustrations. 59pp. 4¼ x 5½.
USO 21102-9 Pa. $1.00

THE MERRY ADVENTURES OF ROBIN HOOD, Howard Pyle. Facsimile of original (1883) edition, finest modern version of English outlaw's adventures. 23 illustrations by Pyle. 296pp. 6½ x 9¼.                              22043-5 Pa. $4.00

TWO LITTLE SAVAGES, Ernest Thompson Seton. Adventures of two boys who lived as Indians; explaining Indian ways, woodlore, pioneer methods. 293 illustrations. 286pp.                                                      20985-7 Pa. $3.00

HOUDINI ON MAGIC, Harold Houdini. Edited by Walter Gibson, Morris N. Young. How he escaped; exposés of fake spiritualists; instructions for eye-catching tricks; other fascinating material by and about greatest magician. 155 illustrations. 280pp. 20384-0 Pa. $2.75

HANDBOOK OF THE NUTRITIONAL CONTENTS OF FOOD, U.S. Dept. of Agriculture. Largest, most detailed source of food nutrition information ever prepared. Two mammoth tables: one measuring nutrients in 100 grams of edible portion; the other, in edible portion of 1 pound as purchased. Originally titled Composition of Foods. 190pp. 9 x 12. 21342-0 Pa. $4.00

COMPLETE GUIDE TO HOME CANNING, PRESERVING AND FREEZING, U.S. Dept. of Agriculture. Seven basic manuals with full instructions for jams and jellies; pickles and relishes; canning fruits, vegetables, meat; freezing anything. Really good recipes, exact instructions for optimal results. Save a fortune in food. 156 illustrations. 214pp. 6⅛ x 9¼. 22911-4 Pa. $2.50

THE BREAD TRAY, Louis P. De Gouy. Nearly every bread the cook could buy or make: bread sticks of Italy, fruit breads of Greece, glazed rolls of Vienna, everything from corn pone to croissants. Over 500 recipes altogether. including buns, rolls, muffins, scones, and more. 463pp. 23000-7 Pa. $4.00

CREATIVE HAMBURGER COOKERY, Louis P. De Gouy. 182 unusual recipes for casseroles, meat loaves and hamburgers that turn inexpensive ground meat into memorable main dishes: Arizona chili burgers, burger tamale pie, burger stew, burger corn loaf, burger wine loaf, and more. 120pp. 23001-5 Pa. $1.75

LONG ISLAND SEAFOOD COOKBOOK, J. George Frederick and Jean Joyce. Probably the best American seafood cookbook. Hundreds of recipes. 40 gourmet sauces, 123 recipes using oysters alone! All varieties of fish and seafood amply represented. 324pp. 22677-8 Pa. $3.50

THE EPICUREAN: A COMPLETE TREATISE OF ANALYTICAL AND PRACTICAL STUDIES IN THE CULINARY ART, Charles Ranhofer. Great modern classic. 3,500 recipes from master chef of Delmonico's, turn-of-the-century America's best restaurant. Also explained, many techniques known only to professional chefs. 775 illustrations. 1183pp. 6⅝ x 10. 22680-8 Clothbd. $22.50

THE AMERICAN WINE COOK BOOK, Ted Hatch. Over 700 recipes: old favorites livened up with wine plus many more: Czech fish soup, quince soup, sauce Perigueux, shrimp shortcake, filets Stroganoff, cordon bleu goulash, jambonneau, wine fruit cake, more. 314pp. 22796-0 Pa. $2.50

DELICIOUS VEGETARIAN COOKING, Ivan Baker. Close to 500 delicious and varied recipes: soups, main course dishes (pea, bean, lentil, cheese, vegetable, pasta, and egg dishes), savories, stews, whole-wheat breads and cakes, more. 168pp. USO 22834-7 Pa. $2.00

COOKIES FROM MANY LANDS, Josephine Perry. Crullers, oatmeal cookies, chaux au chocolate, English tea cakes, mandel kuchen, Sacher torte, Danish puff pastry, Swedish cookies — a mouth-watering collection of 223 recipes. 157pp.
22832-0 Pa. $2.25

ROSE RECIPES, Eleanour S. Rohde. How to make sauces, jellies, tarts, salads, potpourris, sweet bags, pomanders, perfumes from garden roses; all exact recipes. Century old favorites. 95pp.
22957-2 Pa. $1.75

"OSCAR" OF THE WALDORF'S COOKBOOK, Oscar Tschirky. Famous American chef reveals 3455 recipes that made Waldorf great; cream of French, German, American cooking, in all categories. Full instructions, easy home use. 1896 edition. 907pp. 6⅝ x 9⅜.
20790-0 Clothbd. $15.00

JAMS AND JELLIES, May Byron. Over 500 old-time recipes for delicious jams, jellies, marmalades, preserves, and many other items. Probably the largest jam and jelly book in print. Originally titled May Byron's Jam Book. 276pp.
USO 23130-5 Pa. $3.50

MUSHROOM RECIPES, André L. Simon. 110 recipes for everyday and special cooking. Champignons à la grecque, sole bonne femme, chicken liver croustades, more; 9 basic sauces, 13 ways of cooking mushrooms. 54pp.
USO 20913-X Pa. $1.25

THE BUCKEYE COOKBOOK, Buckeye Publishing Company. Over 1,000 easy-to-follow, traditional recipes from the American Midwest: bread (100 recipes alone), meat, game, jam, candy, cake, ice cream, and many other categories of cooking. 64 illustrations. From 1883 enlarged edition. 416pp.
23218-2 Pa. $4.00

TWENTY-TWO AUTHENTIC BANQUETS FROM INDIA, Robert H. Christie. Complete, easy-to-do recipes for almost 200 authentic Indian dishes assembled in 22 banquets. Arranged by region. Selected from Banquets of the Nations. 192pp.
23200-X Pa. $2.50

*Prices subject to change without notice.*
Available at your book dealer or write for free catalogue to Dept. GI, Dover Publications, Inc., 180 Varick St., N.Y., N.Y. 10014. Dover publishes more than 150 books each year on science, elementary and advanced mathematics, biology, music, art, literary history, social sciences and other areas.